MEDSPA MARKETING

MASTERY

PROVEN ONLINE STRATEGIES TO GROW YOUR AESTHETICS PRACTICE

BY JENNIFER CREGO

DEDICATION

This book is dedicated to all of the hardworking aestheticians, medspa owners, and practitioners working to help people feel more confident about their appearance. I hope this book gives you the tools to reach more patients who need your help and grow your aesthetic practice beyond your wildest dreams.

I would also like to thank my loving family. Jon, Aven, and the whole extended gang, thank you for your unwavering support and encouragement.

SPECIAL BONUSES FOR READERS

Thank you for purchasing your copy of Medspa Marketing Mastery. Your purchase includes several free resources that are available to immediately download and put to work for your practice. To get access to all of the free resources offered in this book, go to:

https://medspamarketingbook.com/free-resources

If you know you're ready for help to uplevel your medical spa's digital marketing, we offer a free Marketing Consultation. It starts with a few questions so that we can conduct a thorough audit of your practice's online presence.

During the consultation, we'll go over what's working and where you have room to improve. If it makes sense, we'll share information about the growth programs we offer at Margott. This is a no-pressure, no-obligation consultation. If that sounds good to you, schedule your complimentary consultation today!

https://gomargott.com/get-started

CONTENTS

INTRODUCTION ....

CHAPTER 1: Start With The Fundamentals Of Marketing ....

CHAPTER 2: A Powerful Brand Identity For Your Med Spa ....

CHAPTER 3: The 3R Medspa Marketing System ....

CHAPTER 4: Developing A Comprehensive Marketing Plan 2

CHAPTER 5: Your Website Is The Heart Of Your Digital Presence 38

CHAPTER 6: Online Reviews Matter More Than Ever.. 48

CHAPTER 7: Streamline, Personalize, & Amplify With Marketing Automation....... 56

CHAPTER 8: The Essentials Of Good Search Engine Optimization...................... 66

CHAPTER 9: Establishing Your Medspa's Authority & Trust With Content............ 80

CHAPTER 10: How To Get Ranked In Google Maps.. 86

CHAPTER 11: Reaching A Wider Audience With Paid Ads....................................... 96

CHAPTER 12: Get Maximum Results With Social Media Marketing 114

CHAPTER 13: Using Video To Enhance Your Medspa's Visibility
& Drive Conversions..125

CHAPTER 14: Engage Clients & Leads With Powerful Email &
SMS Communications.. 137

CHAPTER 15: Optimize Your Online Presence For Today's Mobile Users 148

CHAPTER 16: Track, Measure, & Quantify To Ensure A Strong ROI.....................154

CHAPTER 17: Staying Compliant With Email & SMS Regulations.........................162

CHAPTER 18: Next Steps To Fast-Track Your Medspa's Marketing Results 169

INTRODUCTION

I know why you're here reading this book right now. I know the restlessness of ambition and hunger to build a successful business. I know the desire to contribute to a family's financial well-being, pour into a team of skilled, hardworking people, make an impact in the community, and serve clients at the highest level.

I see you, fellow business owner, and I'm happy you're here.

In this book, I will share how you can utilize digital marketing to bring more potential clients to your med spa pre-positioned to buy, increase booked appointments for you and your staff, and grow your business to record heights.

It's an exciting time to be in the medical aesthetics industry. A new concept in the 90s, med spas didn't really become mainstream until the early 2000s, coincidentally around the same time the internet became more widely accessible.

As the internet and aesthetics matured, the med spa industry experienced explosive growth. Maybe because so many of us were desperate for the magical outcomes of cosmetic treatments combined with skilled practitioners or because the internet opened a new gateway to reach people at home, especially once social media arrived. Whatever the reason, the med spa industry boomed, showing no signs of slowing down soon.

As demand grew, so did the competition. Med spas discovered it wasn't enough to launch a medical spa and wait for new clients to call. As competition intensified, digital marketing became essential for med spas to establish their authority, build their brand and community, increase trust and credibility, and of course, drive sales.

In today's market, successful medical spas recognize the importance of building a comprehensive online presence across multiple platforms, which requires digital marketing. I believe one of the most challenging aspects of developing your online presence is that online marketing is a race.

If your competitors are marketing at an elite level, and many are these days, your med spa simply won't be able to keep up if you're marketing at a beginner level. Alternatively, suppose you're marketing at an elite level and differentiating your brand from your competition. In that case, you will attract the right audience to your practice and leave your competitors in the dust.

Through my work with medical spas over the years, I understand your daily challenges. I've pinpointed a few of the most common ones:

- Potential new clients are frequently "no show" for their consultation appointments.
- Many of your new clients are from referrals, and while referrals are fantastic, it's not a predictable way to acquire new clients.
- You're trying to grow, but you need more appointments before you can hire another aesthetician, or you already have enough aestheticians, but they're not booked to capacity.

- Your front desk staff handles calling patients and prospects manually, from new inquiries to appointment reminders.
- An aesthetician, support staff member, or someone on the team is responsible for your med spa's social media posting, but you're pretty sure they don't have any experience in strategic content creation or branding.
- Your office manager tried running Google Ads a while back, and you didn't see one lead from them.
- There is never enough time in the day to be the practitioner, business owner, or boss you want to be while trying to figure out how to increase leads through trial and error.
- Your competitors appear at the top of the page in Google searches while you're stuck on page two, even though you know your services and team are far superior.

Can you relate? The good news is that it doesn't have to be this way. Instead, I want you to experience the growth of your med spa with joy and confidence, and I bet you want that too.

Imagine...

- Being the #1 med spa in your area—you know it, your patients know it, and your competitors certainly know it too.
- Doubling your sales with a steady stream of both new and repeat patients.
- A full staff of committed, skilled aestheticians and practitioners happy to work at their capacity.
- Spending your time exactly as you want to, whether that means more time with your family or more time to build your empire.

It's possible, and this book will show you how. In the following chapters, we'll lay the foundation to:

- Map out your online marketing plan with my proven 3R Medspa Marketing System.

- Understand website conversion fundamentals to ensure your website converts visitors into consultations and new appointments.

- Improve your website's visibility so you can rank on page one for your most important keywords.

- Connect more deeply with your established and potential clients to increase your know, like, and trust factors, ultimately leading to increased sales.

- Discover how to budget for growth to maximize your marketing efforts without spending more than necessary.

- Learn how to track, measure and quantify your online marketing tactics to ensure your investment generates a strong return.

- And much, much more!

I'm beyond excited to go through this journey with you. I'll share the exact marketing strategies that have helped medical spa owners, just like you, double or triple their sales.

But first, who am I, and why should you listen to me?

Before we go any further, I want to give a brief introduction. My name is Jennifer Crego, and I'm the founder of Margott, a digital marketing agency specializing in med spa marketing, and Marketeer+, our sales and marketing platform designed to maximize lead flow for med spas and other aesthetics businesses.

I've been fully immersed in the online world since 2003. Before starting my marketing agency, I was the Director of Business Development for an Internet Retailer 100 company. I spent over twelve years honing my craft to leverage highly effective marketing strategies that delivered qualified leads to our business development endeavors.

Quite possibly more important than my expertise is my commitment to helping businesses grow. I steadfastly believe in the power of entrepreneurship for ourselves and our communities. I fully admit that I have a special allegiance to women-led organizations. When it comes to med spas, this middle-aged woman who is acne-prone and deals with hyperpigmentation is eternally grateful for the work you do. Some people think it's vanity, but I know the truth. Your work improves lives! 🙏

With my team at Margott (predominantly women who also use med spa services), we've helped businesses generate millions of dollars in leads and closed sales. Our mission for every med spa we work with is to make them the #1 med spa in their local area. I initially developed my 3R Medspa Marketing System as our internal process to do just that—more about that in the following chapters.

Of course, I'd love to work with you as a client, but that's not what this book is about. I'm confident that if you take action and implement the digital marketing strategies described in this book, you'll see massive growth in your practice.

Let's get to it.

CHAPTER 1

START WITH THE
FUNDAMENTALS OF MARKETING

Before diving into online marketing and crafting your digital marketing plan, I want to review the marketing fundamentals.

Through my interactions with medical spas and various aesthetics businesses, I've noticed that many overlook the marketing fundamentals and immediately jump into implementing tactics. They often have thoughts on these things but haven't taken the time to get clear on them.

You might be tempted to skip this chapter if you're an established med spa. I encourage you to go through it and review your fundamentals anyway. You must be clear on the marketing fundamentals to develop a solid foundation for your medical spa's marketing.

So, what does "marketing fundamentals" even mean, and how do we get clear on it? Let's take a closer look.

Marketing Fundamentals

"Marketing fundamentals" encompass the three core components that form the backbone of any marketing strategy.

- Message (what)
- Market (who)
- Media (how)

To grow your medical spa successfully, you must have a unique message, a precisely defined market, and media focused on those essential details.

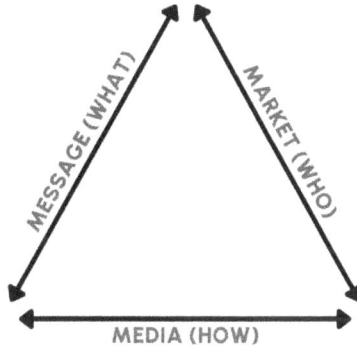

Message

Your unique message differentiates your practice from your competitors. It highlights what makes your medical spa unique and why clients should choose your med spa over the competition.

As you think about this, list a minimum of three differentiators for your medical spa. Each item on the list doesn't have to be 100% unique to your practice and no one else's. However, the combination of the differentiators should be unique to your practice.

Examples of Potential Differentiators

Location: Are you located in a highly desirable or convenient area?

Services: Do you offer treatments that other med spas in your area don't?

Technology: Does your med spa fully embrace technology, judging from the tools you use for managing your practice to the most advanced machines?

Staff: Are your aestheticians all master aestheticians or highly trained or skilled in another way that you can highlight?

One quick note: Good customer service isn't a differentiating factor; it's just doing good business. However, providing your clients with a significantly elevated experience could be a differentiator.

Creating a list of three or more differentiators can be challenging, especially if you're trying to do it independently. You may want to talk to your staff or even a few clients to get ideas.

Ask Yourself: What do we do differently from competing medical spas?

Market

Understanding your market, or ideal client, is an indispensable step in the success of your med spa. It goes beyond a simple desire to serve anyone seeking to enhance their appearance.

While your med spa undoubtedly can help numerous individuals on their journey to self-improvement, it is essential to hone in on your target market. It doesn't mean you can't offer your services to anyone who needs them, but that you're focusing on your ideal clients so that your messaging speaks directly to them.

One way to pinpoint your market is to evaluate your current clients. Analyze 25 of your best patients, focusing on those who made substantial purchases, contributed to higher profit margins, and expressed genuine satisfaction with your services. In that case, you'll discover unique characteristics that define these exceptional clients. Dig deeper into their profiles and consider their residential location, income level, and how they found your service offerings.

Knowing your target audience enhances your marketing efforts and enables you to refine your overall business strategy. With a clear understanding of their unique characteristics, you can optimize various aspects of your med spa, including service offerings, customer experience, and even the ambiance of your facility.

By catering to your ideal clients' specific desires and preferences, you can create an environment that resonates deeply with them, fostering loyalty and long-term relationships.

Ask yourself: Who is my target market?

Media

Once you have identified your market and fine-tuned your message, you can start thinking about media. To determine the most effective media for you, consider where to reach your *ideal* clients.

Clearly, the internet is a great "media" for connecting with your ideal client who is proactively in the market for your services. Throughout the remainder of this book, I'll explain the various Internet marketing channels and how you can use them to connect with your target audience.

The tactics (pay-per-click, SEO, social media, email marketing, etc.) fall into the "media" category. If you focus solely on the media or tactics, you will likely fail regardless of how well-selected that media is. Invest the time and energy in your message and figure out who your market is. Doing this will make ALL of your media choices vastly more effective.

Ask yourself: What do my ideal clients do online, and where do they do it?

Understanding Client Needs & Desires

By understanding the needs and desires of your med spa clients, you can create marketing and sales strategies more likely to resonate with your target audience. Knowing your client's needs and desires also helps you provide the kind of treatment experience your clients seek.

Of course, med spa clients have a wide range of needs and desires, but some of the most common include:

Looking Younger and More Refreshed: Many med spa clients seek ways to improve their appearance and reduce the visible signs of aging. This may include skin tightening treatments, dermal fillers, and laser resurfacing treatments.

Improving Their Skin Health: Med spa clients may also want to improve their skin health. This may include acne treatments, hyperpigmentation treatments, and anti-aging treatments.

Losing Weight or Body Fat: Some med spa clients may be looking for ways to lose weight or body fat. This may include treatments such as CoolSculpting®, laser liposuction, and body contouring.

Reducing Stress and Anxiety: Med spa clients may want to reduce stress and anxiety. This may include IV therapy, massage therapy, and acupuncture.

Boosting Their Energy Levels: Med spa clients may focus on ways to increase their energy levels. This may include IV therapy, vitamin infusions, and NAD+ therapy.

In addition to these specific needs, med spa clients generally desire a safe, comfortable, and effective treatment experience. They want to feel confident they are in good hands with experienced and qualified professionals. They also want to trust that the treatments they receive will be effective and will deliver the results they are looking for.

Keep your clients and potential clients' needs and desires in mind while we go through the following chapters in this book. *Everything* comes back to those essential details.

CHAPTER 2

A POWERFUL BRAND IDENTITY FOR YOUR MED SPA

In today's competitive medical spa industry, having a solid brand identity is crucial for success. A well-crafted brand sets your med spa apart from the competition and establishes trust, credibility, and loyalty among your target audience. Whether you're a seasoned industry professional or just starting your med spa journey, this chapter will help you create a compelling brand that captivates your clients and elevates your business.

At a fundamental level, your med spa's brand should ensure it doesn't turn clients off. Think of how you feel when you meet a stranger on the sidewalk. You won't feel safe and confident if they seem sketchy to you. But if you meet someone who seems friendly and polite, you probably feel very comfortable.

That's exactly how your brand works. It evokes both negative and positive feelings that people have about your practice. When branding is off, it can feel like you're spinning your wheels on marketing and not getting the traction you expect. But when you have a solid brand identity, the benefits are exponential.

The Importance of Branding in Digital Marketing

A powerful brand identity plays a vital role in the success of medical spas for several reasons. First and foremost, in today's competitive marketplace, where the popularity of med spas has skyrocketed, it has become increasingly important for practices to stand out. By developing a well-defined brand, you can create a unique identity for your medical spa that distinguishes you from your competitors and positions you as the preferred choice for your target audience.

A strong brand helps build trust and credibility with potential clients. When clients are familiar with a brand and confident in its reputation, they are more likely to choose that particular med spa over others. This helps improve customer loyalty, increase lead generation, and elevate sales, often even increasing referrals.

Surprisingly, some medical spas overlook the influence of a strong brand on pricing. In an attempt to offer competitive rates for cosmetic procedures, they might undervalue the importance of brand perception. However, a trusted and reputable brand has the power to command a premium price. Clients often pay more for treatments from a brand they trust and believe in.

A robust brand identity is essential for medical spas to thrive in the competitive med spa industry. Investing in branding is a strategic decision that can yield significant long-term benefits for any medical spa.

Key Elements of a Successful Medical Spa Brand

Creating a successful medical spa brand requires careful attention to several factors. The goal is to create a brand that stands out from the competition and attracts your target audience. Everything else in this book, from tactics to channels, is based on first having a solid brand foundation.

The critical elements of a successful medical spa brand are:

Clear and Unique Positioning: A medical spa brand should have a clear and unique positioning in the market. This means that your medical spa should be known for something specific, such as offering a particular type of treatment, using a specific technology, or having a certain atmosphere. This goes back to the messaging we went over in the last chapter.

Strong Brand Identity: A strong brand identity means having both a clear visual and verbal identity. Your med spa's visual identity includes things like your logo and color palette. Your verbal identity includes written or spoken elements like a tagline or mission statement.

Positive Reputation: It's so important for a medical spa brand to have a positive reputation, meaning your practice should be known for providing high-quality services and products and for offering a good customer service experience. And, of course, this comes through loud and clear in your online reviews.

Effective Marketing: An effective marketing strategy is crucial. This means using a variety of marketing channels to reach your target audience and promote your services and products. An effective marketing strategy is never about using one marketing channel—that would be like putting on pants and considering yourself fully dressed.

Excellent Customer Service: As previously mentioned, good customer service isn't a differentiator for your medical spa or any business. People expect excellent customer service as a baseline. For med spas, you're responsive to patient needs and concerns and should go the extra mile to ensure they're satisfied with their experience.

A Commitment to Continuous Improvement: In the aesthetics industry, innovation is vital. Being committed to continuous improvement means constantly looking for ways to improve your med spa's services, products, and marketing strategies.

A Strong Team of Professionals: From aestheticians to injectors and support staff, a medical spa's brand requires a fantastic team of professionals. Your staff should be knowledgeable, experienced, and passionate about providing exceptional outcomes and a top-notch client experience.

It's essential to recognize that building a successful brand takes time. Patience is key as you work toward establishing a strong presence in the medical spa industry. Results won't materialize overnight, but you will gradually see the fruits of your efforts by persistently delivering value and maintaining a consistent brand image.

Define Your Med Spa Brand

To define your brand, start by reflecting on and answering the questions below to gain clarity and direction in developing a compelling brand identity for your med spa. Remember to consistently and authentically communicate your brand identity across all touchpoints. This strengthens your connection with clients and helps to differentiate you in the competitive med spa industry.

How do you want your patients to perceive your med spa?

Envision how you want your clients to perceive your medical spa. Do you want to be considered luxurious, trustworthy, caring, or cutting-edge? Define the key attributes that align with your brand identity goals.

What is your brand's personality?

Determine the personality traits that align with your med spa's brand identity. Is your brand professional, friendly, sophisticated, or approachable? Consider how this personality will be reflected in your messaging, visual elements, and customer interactions.

What is your brand's visual identity?

Explore the visual elements that will represent your brand. This includes logo, color palette, typography, and overall design aesthetic. Ensure these elements align with your brand's personality and appeal to your target audience.

How do you want your clients to feel during and after their experience at your med spa?

Consider the emotions you want to evoke in your clients: do you want them to feel pampered, rejuvenated, empowered, or confident? Understanding the desired emotional impact will guide the creation of a memorable and impactful brand identity.

By addressing these essential aspects, you can craft a memorable and impactful brand identity beyond mere recognition. Ultimately, a well-defined brand that resonates with your target audience becomes a powerful driver of success for your med spa. It sets you apart from competitors, establishes trust, and positions your practice as the go-to med spa in your area, leading to growth, profitability, and a thriving reputation.

CHAPTER 3
THE 3R MEDSPA MARKETING SYSTEM

A big challenge with digital marketing is that people often underestimate the value of some marketing elements and put too much emphasis on parts that don't work on their own. Online marketing is like building a web. Each of the marketing channels works together for the best results. Some channels can be effective on their own, but most need the support of the other channels to be truly effective.

Another challenge I see is when newer medical spas jump into marketing at a level that isn't right for their business in their current position. I created the 3R Medspa Marketing System with three levels of marketing that each builds on the last. Start with level one if you're a newer or smaller med spa. You will need all three levels to compete if you're an established med spa in a competitive market.

Let's go through each level of the 3R Medspa Marketing System to give you an overview of how it works. In the following chapters, I'll go into more detail about each element to provide you with everything you need to implement the system for your practice.

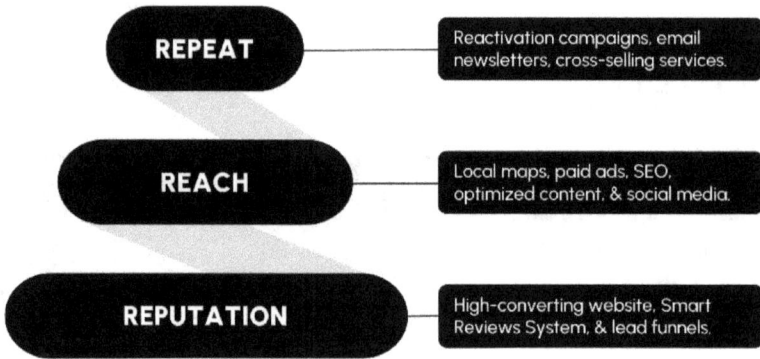

REPEAT — Reactivation campaigns, email newsletters, cross-selling services.

REACH — Local maps, paid ads, SEO, optimized content, & social media.

REPUTATION — High-converting website, Smart Reviews System, & lead funnels.

Level 1: Reputation

Reputation is the foundation of any business, but it's absolutely crucial for med spas. I know I'm preaching to the choir when I tell you that trust is paramount for potential clients seeking treatments to enhance their appearance and well-being. But I think medical spa owners often don't understand what's involved in gaining trust online.

Of course, people will be more comfortable trusting you or your practitioners once they've had a consultation, but there needs to be a level of trust before someone reaches out to schedule an appointment. The Reputation level addresses that need.

A Professional Website

The first step to establishing trust and a good reputation is a professional website. Can your medical spa function without a professional website? Sure, but a professional, high-converting website supports a med spa's reputation more than you might realize.

When someone visits your website for the first time, they form a first impression of your business in less than one second. They're taking in your brand personality, how attractive your website is, and if it loads quickly. Then in half a second, they've already formed their opinion. The shocking part is that they're not just judging your website. They're judging your ENTIRE practice on their first impression. It's alarming, I know!

I explain this to clients by comparing your website to people. Imagine you're hiring a new aesthetician for your med spa, and you interview two candidates. The first candidate arrives for their interview a few minutes early, well-dressed, and prepared for the interview. The second candidate arrives a few minutes late, looking disheveled, unorganized, and unprepared. Based on those things alone to form your first impression, which candidate would you trust more?

Your website is a digital representative of your med spa, and it works similarly to hiring candidates for a job. When potential clients visit your website, they are essentially "interviewing" your med spa to see if it meets their expectations and gains their trust. Just as first impressions matter in a job interview, they are equally crucial for your website's effectiveness in attracting and retaining clients.

In the competitive landscape of med spas, a well-presented website can give you an edge over other med spas with poorly designed or outdated sites. Potential clients are more likely to choose your med spa if your website conveys professionalism, trustworthiness, and a commitment to providing excellent aesthetic services.

Positive Online Reviews

Positive reviews and a solid online reputation instill confidence in potential clients that the med spa is reliable, competent, and provides high-quality services. Many individuals consider online reviews and testimonials essential to their decision-making process.

Positive reviews act as social proof, assuring potential clients that others have had positive experiences at the med spa. Conversely, negative reviews can significantly harm a med spa's reputation and deter potential clients.

Marketing Automation

An attentive and organized lead process is instrumental in increasing a potential client's trust in the medical spa treatments they inquired about. It creates a positive impression of the company's professionalism, responsiveness, and commitment to meeting client needs.

When a potential client inquires about treatment, a positive experience reflects professionalism, instilling confidence that they are dealing with a reputable and reliable med spa. Good customer service is essential, but we expect that everywhere. You can design your clients' experience with your practice; marketing automation can help you do that seamlessly.

Level 2: Reach

With the foundation in place, it's time to add the next level to our marketing stack. Level 2 is all about reach. In marketing, "reach" refers to the number of existing or potential clients exposed to your marketing message, advertisement, or promotional content. The goal of increasing your med spa's reach is to expand visibility, create awareness about your services, and ultimately attract more people to your med spa's treatments and offers.

The bulk of our ongoing marketing efforts is to increase your reach. The key to expanding your reach is to approach each marketing channel as one part of the process. Each channel on its own is much less effective than the channels are together. I think of marketing channels like spokes in a bicycle tire. Each spoke leads to the hub, your business, but your website is your business online. If we were to remove some of the spokes, the tire would be significantly less stable.

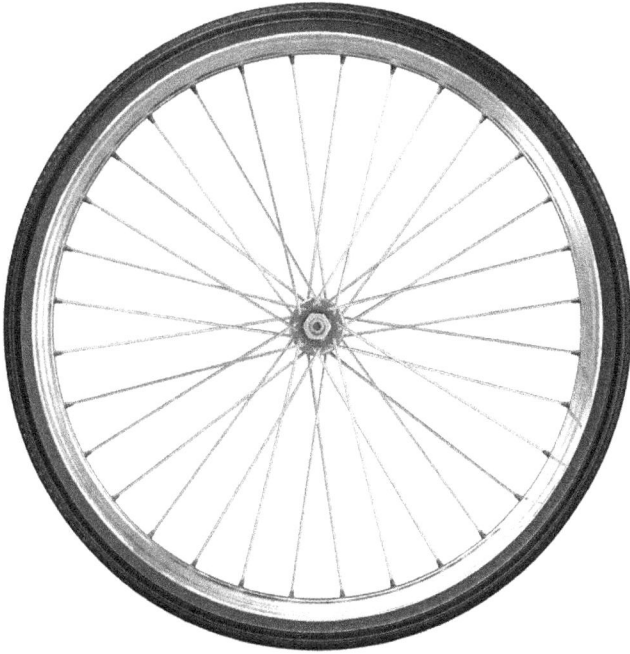

In the same way, your medical spa needs each marketing channel to ensure the stability of your marketing efforts and benefit from an omnipresent approach. By maintaining a balanced and multi-faceted approach to marketing, you can enhance your overall reach, engage with a broader audience, and establish a more robust and resilient presence in your local market.

In the upcoming chapters, I'll cover each digital marketing channel included in the Reach level of the 3R Medspa Marketing System in more detail. For now, here's a short list of the included marketing channels:

- Search Engine Optimization
- Optimized Content
- Google Maps Optimization
- Paid Ads
- Social Media

You don't have to utilize all the marketing channels to have a successful marketing strategy, but you must use as many as it takes to create a comprehensive online presence.

Level 3: Repeat

In Level 1, you'll focus on establishing a solid foundation for your med spa's online presence. Moving on to Level 2, you'll take your marketing efforts to the next level by leveraging multiple marketing channels to increase your reach and attract new clients. In Level 3, it's time to maximize revenue by increasing sales to your existing clients.

In Level 3, you'll use email marketing, SMS, and client data to achieve your objectives. Whether you're developing a reactivation campaign to bring inactive clients back to your treatment rooms or targeted email campaigns to keep your existing clients informed about new services, promotions, or exclusive offers, these communication methods increase sales.

By analyzing your client data and understanding their preferences and needs, you can offer relevant services or products that enhance their experience while increasing the lifetime value of each client. This part of the marketing strategy focuses on optimizing revenue generation by nurturing relationships with existing clients, encouraging repeat business, and providing exceptional service that leads to positive referrals.

When you combine all three levels of your marketing efforts, you create a comprehensive approach that propels your med spa toward sustained growth and success.

The 3R Medspa Marketing System

Digital marketing can be overwhelming, especially for those new to it. But the 3R Medspa Marketing System is designed to help you avoid overwhelm and confusion. But take it one step at a time. Let's go over the three levels one more time:

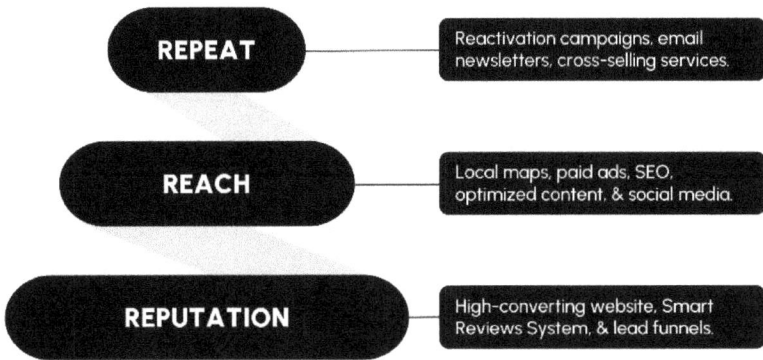

Level 1: Reputation

- High-Converting Website
- Smart Reviews System
- Marketing Automation

Level 2: Reach

- Search Engine Optimization
- Content Marketing
- Google Maps Optimization
- Paid Advertising
- Social Media
- Video Marketing

Level 3: Repeat

- Reactivation Campaigns
- Email Newsletters
- Cross-Selling Services

In the next chapter, we'll create your marketing plan based on your unique growth goals and budget. Then your marketing plan will be your action plan going forward. Let's get started!

CHAPTER 4

DEVELOPING A COMPREHENSIVE MARKETING PLAN

We've gone over your med spa's fundamentals, your brand identity, and the 3R Medspa Marketing System. Now it's time to develop a marketing plan to support your medical spa's growth goals.

A marketing plan is a roadmap to success. We look at where your med spa is now and where you want to go. Then, the marketing plan is simply a map that documents how to get from point A to point B. The key is to follow the map. Don't go rogue! Trust the process, and you'll get where you want to go.

By the end of this chapter, you'll have a marketing plan mapped out for your med spa, and you'll be ready to dive into each element of the 3R Medspa Marketing System.

Step 1 = Level 1: Reputation

First, you'll want to look at where your med spa is now. Honestly evaluate your med spa's position and reputation. If you already have a high-converting website, amazing online reviews, and dialed-in marketing automation, then you're ready for Level 2. If your med spa doesn't have a glowing online reputation, then Level 1 will be where your action plan starts.

Step 2 = Level 2: Reach

As mentioned, most marketing activities fall into the Reach level. This is where the rubber meets the road. From Google Maps and organic search engine optimization to email marketing, social media, and paid ads, there's a lot to consider. That's why it's so important to have a plan. A well-crafted marketing plan encompassing several online opportunities helps you get the most out of your marketing efforts.

Successful med spas don't rise to the top by implementing one marketing channel. The key is leveraging multiple marketing channels to give your medical spa omnipresence. This book will help you do exactly that.

Digital Marketing Channels

There are several marketing channels to explore at the Reach level. In this chapter, I'll briefly cover the marketing channels available to you so that you understand what they are and how they work. Each marketing channel brings unique value to your marketing plan, and this overview will help you see how they can work for your business.

1. Search Engine Optimization
2. Optimized Content
3. Google Maps Optimization
4. Paid Ads
5. Social Media

Search Engine Optimization

Search Engine Optimization (SEO) is enhancing the visibility of your medical spa on popular search engines within the organic search results. This strategic process aims to make your listing prominently appear when people search online for the cosmetic treatments you provide.

Before we dive deeper into SEO, let's clarify search engine optimization (SEO) vs. search engine marketing (SEM). There are three types of SEM, and organic SEO is just one of them.

The three types of search engine marketing are:

- **Advertising/Sponsored Listings:** These are paid ads, typically at the top of the search engine results page. Advertisers can bid on this ad space for their desired keywords to obtain priority placement in search engines.
- **Organic SEO:** These are the listings in the body of the search engine results page, and they make up most of the listings on the page.
- **Local SEO:** These are the listings shown below or next to the map on the search engine results page. Map listings are typically right between the paid ads and the organic listings.

Search engine optimization focuses on making your website appear in organic and map listings. These listings get most of the clicks from searchers. Studies have shown that approximately 70-80% of searchers click on organic (non-paid) or local search results rather than paid ones.

When most people think of "online marketing," they think of search engine optimization. However, you will see that SEO is only one small piece of the MUCH BIGGER online marketing puzzle for med spa owners.

Local SEO

Local SEO is a critical digital marketing strategy for med spas and any other local B2C business. It's focused on making a company more prominent in local search queries, especially those with location-specific intent, such as "near me" searches.

The primary goal is to ensure that when potential clients search for med spa services or treatments within their vicinity, your practice prominently appears in the search results, increasing the likelihood of attracting local clients. Claiming and optimizing your Google Business Profile (GBP) is fundamental to local SEO. This profile appears in Google Maps and Google's local search results, providing essential information about your med spa, including location, contact details, business hours, and customer reviews.

When you optimize your GBP with accurate details, attractive visuals, and compelling descriptions, you increase the likelihood of your med spa moving up the ranks in Google.

Local SEO includes more than GBP optimization, but your GBP significantly impacts your online presence. You must also optimize your website for local keywords, build local citations and backlinks, and manage your online reviews. The more you embrace local SEO, the more empowered your medical practice is to stand out in the competitive local landscape and establish a robust online presence in your community.

Paid Advertising

Now that we have reviewed SEO, let's discuss search engine marketing or pay-per-click (PPC) advertising. PPC marketing is a great way to get your medical spa's website to appear at the top of the search engines almost immediately, driving qualified traffic to your website.

Google and Bing both have paid programs that allow you to buy visibility of your business. Your listings associated with specific keywords are then placed in designated areas of their search engines.

There are three significant benefits of PPC advertising:

- Your keyword listings will appear on search engines almost immediately
- You only have to pay when someone clicks on your listing - hence the term "pay-per-click" marketing
- You can get your ad to show up on national terms in the areas/cities in which you operate

PPC marketing works on an auction system similar to that of eBay. You simply choose your keywords and propose a bid of what you are willing to pay for each click.

Several factors determine placement, which will be discussed in detail in the Paid Ads chapter. But, in the broadest sense, the one willing to pay the most per click will be rewarded the top position in the search engines, while the second-most will be in the second position, etc.

Another aspect of search engine marketing is retargeting. It's a strategic digital advertising technique to reach potential clients who have previously shown interest in your med spa's services but have not yet converted into clients. We display targeted ads to these potential clients across various online platforms to re-engage and encourage them to take further action—more on retargeting later.

Social Media Marketing

There is a lot of buzz around social media (Instagram, Facebook, TikTok, YouTube, Twitter, LinkedIn, Pinterest, etc.), and it's not hard to see why. According to Forbes, approximately 4.9 billion people use social media in 2023. Just look at the staggering statistics:

- YouTube has at least 2.5 billion monthly active users in 2023
- YouTube viewers watch over 1 billion hours of video each day
- Instagram has 2 billion monthly active users
- The median age of Facebook's advertising audience is 32 years old
- TikTok has over 1.6 billion active users, with over 116.5 million located in the USA
- TikTok has seen a 12.6% increase in reported ad reach, equal to about 122 million people

Many of the aesthetic businesses I meet are utilizing social media. Sometimes, it's the only marketing channel they're using. Social media is a fantastic way to connect with established and potential patients. By doing so, you can solidify and maintain existing relationships, remain top-of-mind, and ultimately increase repeat and referral business.

We'll dive deeper into social media marketing later in this book to help med spas get the most out of their social media efforts.

Video Marketing

Video marketing and social media go hand in hand. If you're not including video in your social media strategy, you're not getting the most out of your social media efforts. Video today is an absolute must!

Millions of people conduct YouTube searches every day. Many medical spa owners are so focused on social media that they completely neglect the opportunities that YouTube provides.

By implementing a video marketing strategy for your practice, you can get additional placement in search results for your keywords, enhance the effectiveness of your SEO efforts, and improve visitor conversion.

Email & SMS Marketing

Like social media marketing, email & SMS marketing is a great way to remain top-of-mind with your clients and increase repeat business and referrals. Compared to other marketing channels, this is by far the most cost-effective way to communicate with your clients.

Email marketing is one of the least utilized marketing channels among med spas. The good news is that your clients and potential clients aren't likely to get many emails (if any!) from your competitors. This is an opportunity too good not to take action on.

With email marketing, you can nurture leads, engage with clients, and incorporate marketing automation to send personalized content based on specific triggers or actions the recipients take. For example, when a user signs up for a newsletter, marketing automation can automatically send a welcome email with relevant information and offers.

Marketing automation is another aspect of digital marketing that you'll learn more about in this book. It uses email and text messaging to streamline and optimize marketing processes, allowing you to deliver targeted and personalized messages to your audience.

Step 3 = Level 3: Repeat

And that's a great segway into Level 3, a pivotal stage in your med spa's growth journey. While Level 2 is all about attracting more clients to your realm, Level 3 focuses on client retention.

In this phase, you'll use email marketing, SMS campaigns, and marketing automation to nurture your audience and foster lasting relationships with your clients. In the process, you're ensuring that your clients are well taken care of, but the Repeat strategy also creates a powerful mechanism for boosting your med spa's sales and increasing your client's lifetime value.

We'll get into the "how" later in this book. For now, you simply need to decide whether you're ready to get started with Repeat strategies or if you need to focus on Reputation or Reach for the time being. If you're not sure, that's ok! It will become more apparent as you navigate the chapters ahead.

Now that you understand each internet marketing channel available, I'll share how you can leverage them to connect with new and established clients and grow your practice.

Where to Start?

With so many options in online marketing channels, where should you start? I firmly believe that a comprehensive marketing plan for an aesthetics practice requires leveraging each of these online marketing opportunities. However, that level of authority and influence can be built over time.

I developed the 3R Medspa Marketing System to make it easy to pinpoint where to start. First, start with Level 1: Reputation. Make sure your website is a conversion-focused website that acts as an online hub for all your marketing efforts. Your med spa website must be set up properly with conversion design strategies, optimized content, and solid technology.

Once you feel comfortable with your practice at that level, you can move to Level 2: Reach. The marketing channels you decide to lean into will depend on your short and long-term goals and budget, which we'll cover in this chapter.

Paid ads will get results faster than other marketing channels. The leads you acquire from paid ads tend to be high-quality because people who click on paid ads are already interested in the cosmetic treatments you offer. Those searchers are typically willing, ready, and able to buy.

Even though paid ads are effective, sometimes medical spas avoid them because they require an ad spend budget. The benefits of paid ads can far outweigh the necessary investment, so I recommend you consider it.

SEO takes longer to see the results. The first few months can seem like you're investing in a losing strategy, but each month builds on the last until you're "suddenly" seeing gains. SEO should be a cornerstone in the marketing plan for all med spas, especially Local SEO. It's that important.

When comparing the advantages and disadvantages of paid ads and SEO, I like to use an analogy that helps explain how they work.

SEO is like buying a home, maybe even a fixer-upper. You're paying a mortgage and investing in home improvements to increase the value of your home. It's a slow, steady process that will pay off over time. The house probably doesn't have all the luxuries you dream of, but it's a solid investment.

Paid ads, on the other hand, are like the luxurious oceanfront house you rented on Airbnb for your vacation. You're not looking for the same long-term return on your investment as your personal home. You want to be wowed while you're on vacation, and you're willing to pay for it. When your vacation is over, and you're no longer paying for the luxurious vacation home, you can no longer access it. Paid ads work the same way.

I hope that helped explain the difference between the expected outcomes of SEO and paid ads. They're not just different marketing channels but totally different approaches to your med spa's growth. Ideally, you could invest in both marketing channels for your med spa. If not, your investment dollars should be spent where they will impact your specific goals most.

That's precisely what we'll be looking at next—your goals!

Your Growth Goals

It's easy to glaze over particular growth goals and just focus on general growth. However, by narrowing your focus to specific objectives, you'll be better positioned to make intelligent decisions for your practice.

Increasing total revenue is the most straightforward goal but certainly not the only metric to focus on. Here are a few examples of growth goals you may want to incorporate into your plan:

- Increase total revenue to $__
- Increase revenue by __%
- Acquire __ new clients in the next quarter
- Increase the average LTV of patients by __%
- Increase your revenue per hour by __%
- Increase your revenue per appointment by __%

I recommend identifying three growth goals you're focusing on at any given time. That doesn't mean you're not measuring other things, but keep just three as your primary focus. Remember to be specific so that you can evaluate your results and easily determine if you're meeting your goals or not. After a few months, if you aren't meeting your goals or heading in that direction, you'll know that you need to troubleshoot to figure out why.

Once you determine the growth goals you want to focus on, you're ready to nail down your marketing budget. Read on to learn how to do that.

Your Marketing Budget

I have seen many businesses determine their marketing budget by their comfort level or a gut feeling on how much they should spend. The truth is, determining your marketing budget is a simple math equation. However, you first need to consider how competitive you want to be.

Years ago, in a simpler time with less competition and online noise, the Small Business Administration (SBA) recommended small businesses with less than $5 million in annual revenue invest 7%-8% of total revenue on marketing. Today, successful business-to-consumer (B2C) companies, like med spas, often invest 14%-17% of their goal gross revenue on marketing, and it's not uncommon for new med spas to invest 20% or more to ramp things up as quickly as possible.

Remember, digital marketing is highly dependent on your competitors. If your competitors spend 15% of their revenue on marketing, it will be challenging to keep up if you're investing 5%. It's like you're running a race; the winner is your area's "go-to" med spa.

So, to determine your marketing budget, you first need to decide on your goal gross revenue and what percentage of your revenue you will allocate to marketing. I call this percentage your "competitive percentage," typically between 10% and 20%. Then, it's just a matter of plugging in the numbers. I'll use 10% in the examples below for easy math.

Goal Gross Revenue * .10 = Total Marketing Budget

For instance, if your goal gross revenue for your med spa is $2 million in revenue annually, to find your recommended marketing budget, simply multiply $2 million by .10. The outcome is how much your practice should invest in marketing.

That is your total marketing budget, which includes more than digital marketing. You may have event expenses, client gifts, local sponsorships, etc., all of which would fall within your budget. Of course, digital marketing requires most of the budget, but you can use one more equation to determine your digital marketing budget.

Total Marketing Budget * .90 = Your Digital Marketing Budget

Let's see some actual numbers with the same $2 million example.

First, total goal gross revenue multiplied by your competitive percentage (Again, I'm using 10% for easy math) equals your total annual marketing budget.

$2,000,000 * .10 = $200,000

Then, your entire marketing budget multiplied by .90 equals your yearly marketing budget designated for digital marketing.

$200,000 * .90 = $180,000

One more formula to break down the budget into a monthly figure. Take your annual digital marketing budget divided by 12, which equals your monthly digital marketing budget.

$180,000 / 12 = $15,000

If this were the med spa you wanted to grow to $2 million in annual sales, you would want to spend $15,000 monthly on your digital marketing efforts.

As you can see, determining your digital marketing budget is a simple formula. You may want to change some factors in the formula, like the competitive percentage and the percentage dedicated to digital marketing. However, the formula still works the same way.

If you'd like to use our online tool with all the percentages already set up, I have a resource for you. Go to https://medspamarketingbook.com/budget-calculator to try it out.

Your Marketing Plan

Now that you have an idea of the marketing channels you may want to include in your marketing plan, you've identified your growth goals, and you've determined your digital marketing budget, it's time to bring it all together.

I love jigsaw puzzles—figuring out which sections of the puzzle to work on first, looking for the nuances in the design to see the patterns in color, trying several different pieces to see if they'll fit, and seeing the whole thing come together one piece at a time. My idea of a great time is a jigsaw puzzle and a true crime podcast.

Developing a digital marketing plan is the same way (minus the true crime podcast). When determining which marketing channels to include in your plan, first look for the biggest bang for your buck, then layer in the channels that could be considered low-hanging fruit. However, you may need to remove a channel or two to stay within budget. Don't worry; you can always add them back into your marketing plan subsequently. Alternatively, you may find that you can add a channel a two.

The following chapters in this book will give you additional details about the marketing channels available to you and how you can leverage them for your med spa practice. Approach your marketing plan as a puzzle to be solved, and you'll see everything start to come together.

CHAPTER 5

YOUR WEBSITE IS THE HEART OF YOUR DIGITAL PRESENCE

Level 1: Reputation

- **High-Converting Website**
- Online Reviews
- Marketing Automation

This book details leveraging digital marketing for your medical spa practice. However, as you learned in the last chapter, it all begins with your med spa's reputation, and that starts with your website. A professional website is the first step for a good reason. Without a well-designed and fully functional website, the following marketing efforts described in this book would be in vain.

I want to emphasize "well-designed and fully functional." Your website must be done well to build credibility and trust with clients and potential clients. That being said, thousands of gorgeous websites aren't doing anything to convert visitors into consultations or booked appointments. Your website has to be more than a pretty face. It needs to work hard for you, and that requires conversion strategies.

The Essential Pages for Your Medical Spa Website

A well-designed medical spa website should include several core pages serving as essential resources for potential clients. By incorporating these pages, your website will effectively provide visitors with the information they need to make informed decisions about your services. These core pages also enhance the user experience by providing the information visitors expect to find on a medical spa website.

Core Pages

1. Home
2. About Us
3. Treatments (Pages for each treatment or treatment category)
4. Blog
5. Schedule an Appointment
6. Contact Us
7. Privacy Policy & Terms of Service

The homepage is often the first page potential clients will see, so making a strong first impression is crucial. The homepage should provide an overview of your med spa, unique selling points, and key services.

The About page tells your med spa's story and sets your practice apart from the competition. It can include your medical spa's history, values, and information about the team, including their qualifications and expertise.

Treatment pages, or treatment category pages, need to describe the treatments or services you offer in detail. Include benefits, duration, price range, and any preparations or aftercare required. High-quality photos or videos can enhance these descriptions too. You want to have pages for each of your services because they will be optimized with different keyword combinations, which I'll explain in the SEO chapter. I recommend including a FAQ section on each Treatment page. This additional information helps potential clients gain confidence in your services, and a big bonus is that FAQs help SEO results too.

An influential blog contains informative content that helps to establish your medical spa as a knowledgeable authority in the industry. Your blog must be regularly updated with new content. This is a critical component of your SEO strategy, helping potential clients find you through search engines. Again, I'll go into more detail about that in an upcoming chapter.

A Schedule an Appointment page is critical for medical spas. Don't get too caught up on "page" here. Your med spa may use a popup for this, and that's just as effective. What's most important is that a user-friendly online booking system lets clients easily schedule appointments at their convenience, enhancing their overall experience with your spa. You can decide whether to offer online booking for all your services or limit them to consultations.

It's essential to make it easy for visitors to get in touch by including your phone number, email address, and location in the footer of your website. That way, the details are available to website visitors no matter what page they're on. However, this practice doesn't replace the need for a Contact page.

A Contact page is where you'll want a contact form for inquiries, but it's much more than that. A contact form is a trust element for website visitors, whether they use it or not. And Google wants websites to have a Contact page, so we don't really need a reason beyond that.

A website's Legal Policy pages are crucial for legal reasons and building trust with your clients and potential clients. They outline how you handle client information and what terms of service clients agree to when using your website or services. Ideally, a medical website will have privacy, terms of service, and disclaimer pages, but a Privacy page is legally required, at the very least.

While the core pages apply to every medical spa website, the following potential pages are only needed if relevant to your practice. That's not to say they're less important. These additional pages are highly beneficial for aesthetic practices.

Potential Additional Pages

1. Specials & Events
2. Before & After Gallery
3. Common Conditions
4. Skincare Products
5. Financing Options
6. In The Press
7. Reviews & Testimonials
8. Careers

Most medical spas can benefit from a Specials & Events page. If your practice doesn't discount, this page can be used to share information about your referral program.

A gallery showcasing high-quality before and after photos is great, but don't let that keep you from putting before and after photos on the Service pages where you know people will be looking. Before and after images offer tremendous social proof, so don't hide them away on a single page.

A Common Conditions page allows your clients to explore your services while they consider what is most important to them. This will enable people to research their options before seeing an aesthetician and can lead to working with clients who are more educated about their desired outcomes. People tend to feel like they've done their due diligence when they dig into information about conditions and the treatments that can help, which delivers clients pre-positioned to buy. Additionally, the common conditions listed on the page are linked to the individual service pages, which is helpful for a website's optimization.

Skincare Products, Financing, and In The Press are clear-cut. Of course, your practice doesn't need a Financing page if you don't offer financing options. Include these pages on your website when relevant to your medical spa.

A separate Reviews or Testimonials page used to be a recommended core page. However, if all your reviews are on one page, there's no way to guarantee that your website visitors will view that page. Alternatively, if you have testimonials on every page, website visitors are guaranteed to see the testimonials on the page they visited. That said, some medical spas like to have a dedicated page in addition to the reviews on each page, which works well. No matter how you approach reviews, having them on your website is an important trust element and social proof.

A Careers page can greatly improve your hiring process. These days, candidates give the companies they work for as much consideration as they give candidates. This page not only allows you to collect resumes 24/7, but it's also where you begin to "sell" your practice to potential hires. Testimonials from your current team members should be included for maximum impact.

Conversion Fundamentals

I believe there are far too many websites on the internet that aren't truly serving businesses in the best way possible, and I don't want you to fall into that trap. As I see it, you can have the best advertising campaigns and search engine optimization or be ranked number one in Google Maps, but if your website isn't set up in a way that converts, it's just slightly better than useless. Ouch!

Your website must be compelling, give users a reason to choose your med spa over the competition, and provide the information they need to quickly feel you're the right med spa practice to call for help. This starts with conversion-focused web design.

Conversion-focused web design refers to the practice of designing and optimizing a website with the primary goal of driving user conversions. A conversion can be any desired action a visitor takes on a website, such as filling out a form to schedule a consultation, calling the business, making a purchase, subscribing to a newsletter, or downloading a resource.

A conversion-focused website's design elements, layout, and content are strategically planned and implemented to guide visitors toward taking these desired actions. The main objective is to create a seamless user experience that encourages visitors to engage with the website and ultimately convert into consultations or booked appointments.

Conversion design could be its own book. Since this is an overview, I'll share some of the essential elements of a conversion-focused website.

Clear & Intuitive Navigation

The website should have a logical and user-friendly navigation structure that lets visitors quickly find what they want and move through the conversion process. For actual conversion design, the navigation menu should only include the pages most relevant to conversions. Everything else is considered a distraction.

Your Primary Contact Details

Your primary contact details are also part of the header navigation. Your website should always show a phone number in the upper right-hand corner of every page. Statistically, people expect the phone number to be there. Remember that every visitor to your website has a different situation and frame of mind. You may have someone on their phone or just leisurely looking to contact you for your med spa services, and it's easy for them to call you.

On the other hand, someone in a work environment may not be able to stop what they are doing and make a phone call without drawing unwanted attention to themselves. In this case, a simple website form to request an appointment helps your website's conversions. Make it easy for people to schedule with you, whether by phone call or a web form.

The rest of your contact details should be in the footer of your website and the Contact page. Google wants this information on every page, which is good for your search results and website visitors interested in your services. It's a win-win!

Strong Calls to Action

Conversion-focused websites use prominent and visually appealing calls to action (CTA) to encourage visitors to take specific steps. CTAs can be in the form of buttons, banners, or text links that clearly communicate what action the visitor should take next. Each page should have only one primary CTA.

Responsive & Mobile-Friendly Design

Conversion-focused web design ensures your website is accessible and visually appealing across different screen sizes and devices. This doesn't mean your website contains the same information in desktop and mobile versions. People visiting your website from a mobile device are in a different state of mind than those browsing your website on a computer. The mobile version of your website should be condensed, fitting the device screen and giving visitors just the information they need. It should integrate with their phone, so all they have to do is press a button to call you.

Proper functionality is crucial. If you've ever tried to complete an online form that wasn't optimized well for mobile, you know exactly how frustrating it can be. If a potential client is interested in your medical spa services, you want to ensure they have a positive experience with your practice from beginning to end. That starts with your website.

Social Media Links

You also want to provide links to your social media profiles. Make it easy for people to engage with your medical spa on your chosen platforms. It helps create a sense of authenticity when your patients see your social media content.

For conversion-focused web design, social media links should be in the footer of your website, not in the header. If social media links are in your header, they're considered "leaks." You've put much effort into getting visitors to your med spa website. Don't invite them to leave your website as soon as they arrive.

Trust Signals

Trust signals show potential clients they can trust you because others trust you. They are incredibly powerful! A large percentage of people give online reviews the same credibility that they give to a personal referral. So, show positive reviews on every page, even if you decide to have a dedicated page for reviews.

Your website design should also include visual elements that indicate you're a credible medical spa. For example, suppose you're accredited with the Better Business Bureau, a certified woman-owned company, a local Chamber of Commerce member, or any professional industry association. In that case, these associations can be shared on your website to support your trustworthiness with patients.

Authentic Images

It's imperative to infuse your company's website with personality, which is primarily achieved with authentic photos and videos. If you can do a professional photo shoot at your practice, it's worth the investment. Whenever possible, showcase your team, treatment rooms, equipment, the office, etc. This allows the visitor to get to know, like, and trust you and your team before they even pick up the phone. I've seen this tactic prove itself time and time again.

Authenticity Converts 10 to 1.

While stock photos are typically an important part of med spa websites, lousy or cheesy ones don't have to be. Beauty culture is constantly evolving. To attract new patients, make sure any stock photos used on your website portray natural, healthy beauty and not highly edited photos of unattainable results.

Compelling & Persuasive Website Content

Your website's content should be persuasive, highlighting the value proposition and benefits of your practice's cosmetic treatments. It should effectively communicate the unique selling points and address visitors' potential concerns or objections.

Compelling content requires empathizing with the reader, positioning your practitioners as authorities on the subject, and including a clear call to action after all, or almost all, blocks of text. Conversion content pulls visitors deeper into your website to learn more about your team members on the About page, discover special offers, and be compelled to take action and call your med spa. Your content helps people know that your med spa is the right place for them to get the outcome they want with various treatments.

Avoid Confusion - Clarity Wins Every Time

When a website visitor lands on your website, your messaging must answer three initial questions:

1. Who are you?
2. What do you do?
3. How can I buy it?

These three questions must be answered within 2-3 seconds of the visitor landing on your website. That doesn't give your website enough time to be clever. Your website messaging must be crystal clear.

Here are a few website headings that sound nice but hurt conversions rather than helping.

"Welcome to our World"

"Explore the Possibilities"

"Unleash Your Potential"

"The Power of Innovation"

These headings don't convey what the business does. If your website visitors have to think to figure out if they're in the right place, you've already lost them. The importance of this element can't be overestimated. It's crucial to the success of your medical spa's website.

A word of caution: Writing copy for a website requires persuasive copywriting. It's entirely different from the academic writing we all learn in school. If you're writing your website copy, forget everything you learned in English 101. Studies have shown that people read about 20% of the content on any web page. Blocks of text must be formatted so that they're skimmable, which means short paragraphs, bulleted lists, and plenty of white space.

The Med Spa Website Framework

It's not enough to simply write good content. For the best outcomes, the content needs to be structured in a specific order that guides website visitors through a logical flow of information.

Through our experience working directly with medical spas, we've developed a conversion-focused framework that works to sell cosmetic treatments and book appointments. The framework is adapted from Donald Miller's StoryBrand methodology, which focuses on clear messaging, building trust, and an overall persuasive web presence.

If you'd like this resource, go to https://medspamarketingbook.com/free-resources to download a copy of our Medspa Website Framework.

CHAPTER 6

ONLINE REVIEWS MATTER MORE THAN EVER

Level 1: Reputation

- High-Converting Website
- **Online Reviews**
- Marketing Automation

The Importance of Online Reviews

Online reviews can significantly impact a med spa's bottom line. Aesthetics companies that collect and manage reviews effectively can use them to attract new customers, increase sales, and improve their online reputation. Conversely, negative reviews can have detrimental effects, dissuading potential patients and potentially harming a med spa's reputation.

The prevalence and importance of online reviews cannot be overstated. In today's digital age, where information is readily accessible, consumers have come to rely on the experiences and opinions of others to guide their purchasing decisions. The fact that 97% of consumers consider customer reviews when making a buying choice speaks volumes about their influence.

The level of trust they have garnered makes online reviews even more compelling. An astounding 88% of consumers place the same level of trust in online reviews as in personal recommendations from their closest friends. This speaks to the immense power of online reviews and their impact on consumer decision-making.

In addition to influencing consumer perception, more reviews can improve your medical spa's visibility in search engine results, increasing your online presence. Google sees reviews as evidence that your medical spa is a relevant option when people are searching for your services. Reviews are an essential aspect of Google's local search algorithm.

Considering the weight consumers assign to online reviews, it's important to recognize their importance for your med spa and actively manage your online reputation. If you're not collecting reviews, you're missing out on a valuable opportunity to grow your practice. By harnessing the power of online reviews, you can position your medical spa for success in today's highly competitive aesthetics market.

Getting Reviews

Now that we've established the importance of reviews, let's discuss how you can get them or get more. You can engage your patients to leave an online review for your med spa in several ways.

One of the easiest ways to increase your positive reviews is by simply asking patients to give you a review when they're checking out of their appointment. Sometimes this can feel too bold for front desk staff, but there are ways to work around that.

I recommend review cards. They are small cards that can be stapled to a receipt or handed to a client when they're checking out. The cards can be any size, from a standard business card to a small postcard.

The key is prioritizing the client's happiness with their experience, not just getting a review. It's a subtle difference, but it matters. The card should include your logo, a short thank you, what to do if they didn't love their experience at your practice, and a message asking for a review with a QR code that links to your preferred review platform.

Another way to increase your reviews is by emailing patients after each treatment. This is best done with automation in your email marketing software. The email would be something like this:

Email Subject: Thank you for your business!

[Patient's Name],

I'm reaching out to thank you for choosing [Medical Spa Name]. We genuinely appreciate your trust in us and hope you had an outstanding experience.

Your opinion matters! I'd like to ask if you would take a quick moment to leave a review for us online. Your feedback can make a huge difference for others looking for similar services.

To leave a review, click the link below, and you'll be directed to select your preferred platform to leave a review.

[Link to Website]

Thank you, again, for choosing [Medical Spa Name] and sharing your feedback. We can't wait to see you again soon! If you have any questions or need assistance, please don't hesitate to contact me by replying to this email or calling us at [Phone Number].

Take care, and stay fabulous!

[Your Name]

[Your Title/Position]

[Medical Spa Name]

Every medical spa is bound to receive reviews at some point, but being intentional about growing your reviews can make a significant difference. By actively seeking and encouraging online reviews, you can shape your med spa's online reputation and increase your online visibility to attract more customers.

Give Clients Options

While Google is the clear leader in online reviews, there are several other places online that shouldn't be ignored. Yes, you want to have a lot of reviews on Google Maps, but Google is also looking at the reviews you have on other websites like Facebook, Yelp, and RealSelf. Diversifying where you're getting reviews looks more authentic than having many reviews in one place.

To facilitate this diversification, you'll want a page on your website with links to various sites where people can write reviews. You don't need many links here, just a few to make the process convenient, but not too many that would be overwhelming.

By offering a few different options, you're accounting for various people. People use different systems. Personally, I'm a big Google user. If you sent me an email or gave me a card that said, "Please write me a review," and provided me with various options, I would head straight to Google to write my review.

However, some people don't have a Google account and aren't active Google users, but maybe they're active on Facebook or big-time Yelp reviewers. They will have active accounts somewhere, and writing a review where they already have an existing account is much easier.

If you only give them one option, Google Maps, for example, but they happen to be a Yelp user without a Google account, they will have to go out of their way to create an account to write a review, which is not likely to happen. But let's say they did decide to create an account. That review won't count much because there's no active profile history. By providing options, the Yelp user with a reputation for writing reviews and who decides to write one for you will make a difference. That review is going to stick as opposed to being filtered.

The easier and more convenient you make it for people, the better. It's going to bode well in your favor.

Proactive Review Management

Monitoring online reviews is essential to managing your med spa's online presence. When you receive a new review, whether it's positive or negative, it's crucial to respond promptly and professionally.

Remember, when someone has written a review, they've invested taken time, our most valuable resource, and invested it in your practice. Acknowledge that and give each reviewer the respect they deserve. That includes your time, or a team member's time, to thank them for the review.

Of course, positive reviews are what we always strive for. They're pretty easy to respond to. You just want to show the reviewer some love and appreciation. Let them know that you're grateful for their kind words. A little personal touch can go a long way, so make your response heartfelt and genuine. Don't forget to invite them to connect if they need anything else. Building a positive relationship is key to keeping clients coming back.

Negative reviews are a different story. In my experience, I've found it's common for med spas to want to ignore poor reviews. Maybe it goes back to the messages we were told as kids, like, "If you don't have something nice to say, don't say anything at all." Or maybe negative reviews feel personal, and you feel deeply wounded, defensive, or angry. It can be challenging, but as a business owner, or the person responsible for your medical spa's online reputation, you must rise above it.

When dealing with a negative review, how you handle it is less important for the specific reviewer you're replying to and more important for prospective patients reading reviews to decide whether or not they should try your medical spa. They don't expect you to have all 5-star reviews. Negative reviews are part of working with people, but they expect you to respond professionally.

And yes, people do read your replies. One of my sisters rarely reads a business's positive reviews. She says the negative reviews and the subsequent responses tell her everything she needs to know. She's a smart lady!

To handle negative feedback like a pro, first, lead with empathy. Put yourself in the client's shoes. Maybe they're unreasonable or just plain wrong, but perhaps they aren't. Try to see the situation objectively.

Start by acknowledging their dissatisfaction and apologizing for any trouble they experienced. It's all about showing that you genuinely care and want to make things right. Whenever possible, try to take the conversation offline. Give them a direct email or phone number to discuss their concerns privately. Doing this shows that you're committed to finding a solution and that their experience matters to you.

Here's an example of a response to a negative review:

Thank you for taking the time to share your concerns regarding your recent experience with [Medical Spa]. We sincerely apologize for the inconvenience and frustration you experienced.

If you would give us a call at [Phone Number], we'd like the opportunity to make things right. We look forward to resolving the situation and regaining your trust.

Turning a disgruntled client into a happy one can make a huge difference in your brand's reputation. But again, even if you can't turn that unhappy situation around, future potential patients are reading your response and judging how you handled the situation. They want to know that if they have a negative experience, you'll treat them respectfully and fairly.

HIPAA Compliance & Reviews

Remaining HIPPA compliant adds a layer of complexity to a medical spa's online reviews. Regardless of the personal details a patient shares in their review, your reply can't include any details that could identify an individual's health condition, treatments, or any other PHI. Be cautious that you don't even confirm the details the patient shares.

Instead, respond in a general and non-specific manner. For example, instead of addressing specific medical situations or treatments, focus on expressing gratitude for the feedback and showing a commitment to addressing any concerns. Provide general information or resources to help the reviewer without revealing personal or sensitive information.

If you have someone on your team responsible for replying to reviews, ensure they are fully trained on HIPAA regulations and understand the importance of maintaining patient privacy. It's also a good idea to establish clear protocols and guidelines for responding to reviews is also a good idea, emphasizing the importance of HIPAA compliance. You can standardize your team's language and approach to ensure consistency and minimize the risk of inadvertently disclosing PHI.

Remember, the key is to prioritize patient privacy and confidentiality while still acknowledging and addressing reviews professionally and meaningfully. Maintaining a strong focus on HIPAA compliance enables you to engage effectively with reviewers while safeguarding sensitive information.

CHAPTER 7

STREAMLINE, PERSONALIZE, & AMPLIFY WITH MARKETING AUTOMATION

Level 1: Reputation

- High-Converting Website
- Online Reviews
- **Marketing Automation**

Introduction to Marketing Automation

Marketing automation uses software to automate repetitive marketing activities, such as email marketing, SMS marketing, and lead nurturing. It involves setting up predefined rules, triggers, and actions to streamline and optimize marketing efforts.

I know that definition of marketing automation probably seems pretty dry. It's a powerful technology-driven marketing tool, but in essence, marketing automation simply delivers the right message to the right person at the right time.

The main goal of marketing automation is to craft seamless and personalized experiences that make clients feel valued, understood, and appreciated. By automating various processes and utilizing customer data, we can deliver messages, recommendations, and offers that genuinely connect with each individual personally.

The ultimate result? Enhanced client satisfaction, which in turn drives customer loyalty, advocacy, and, of course, revenue for your medical spa. By leveraging marketing automation, we can create a nurturing and tailored journey that leaves a lasting impression on every client, fostering strong and enduring relationships.

It's clear that marketing automation enhances the client experience, but it also impacts the bottom line genuinely. Studies have shown that online inquiries have the best closing rate when they are responded to within 5 minutes. After that, the 5-minute "Golden Window" closes, and the closing rate decreases exponentially.

For most busy med spas, expecting an immediate response is not feasible. Marketing automation can help you achieve that fairly effortlessly, though. Automated workflows can be set up to reply to inquiries immediately, even if it's a simple acknowledgment thanking the person for the inquiry.

We live in an instant gratification world, and while everything can't be instantaneous, the faster we can meet the potential client's needs, the better. That's why online booking and video consultations are valuable for med spas.

Types of Marketing Automation

Marketing automation is introduced in the first level of the 3R Medspa Marketing System, but it's integral to all three levels. It offers med spas a powerful and efficient way to engage with clients, nurture relationships, and drive business growth. There are countless ways your med spa can use marketing automation to streamline your marketing efforts while enhancing your client's experience. I'll cover the six types of automation that I like to implement or refine first.

Sales Inquiries

Again, timeliness is crucial when it comes to sales inquiries. If you don't take immediate action, the potential client is moving on to look at your competitors. I know it's unrealistic to expect your staff to reply to inquiries immediately, but with the help of automation, the inquirer can feel like they've received immediate attention. It's all about conversational messaging that helps move the person along in the buying or scheduling process.

Appointment Reminders & Follow-Ups

Managing appointments is critical to running a med spa. Email and SMS automation enables you to send automated appointment reminders and follow-ups, reducing the risk of no-shows and improving overall client satisfaction. By integrating your scheduling software with your email & SMS marketing platform, you can effortlessly automate the process, ensuring that clients receive timely reminders and post-treatment check-ins.

Welcome & Onboarding Email Sequences

A well-crafted welcome sequence is an excellent opportunity to make a positive first impression on new patients. Through email automation, you can create a series of emails that guide new clients through the onboarding process, introduce them to your services, share success stories, and offer incentives or discounts. A warm and informative welcome sequence provides several benefits, one being it strengthens your connection with new patients from the beginning, which is extremely valuable.

Upselling & Cross-Selling Opportunities

Email and SMS automation can be leveraged to promote additional services or products to existing clients. You can design automated email campaigns that suggest complementary or upgraded services by analyzing clients' past treatments or purchase histories. This approach increases revenue and enhances the client experience by providing tailored recommendations. I'll go into this in more detail later in this book once we're at the Repeat level.

Post-Treatment Care & Follow-Ups

Imagine how delighted your clients would be to receive a text a day or two after their treatment to check on them. Demonstrating care for your client's well-being after treatment is crucial for building trust and loyalty. Marketing automation allows you to send post-treatment care instructions, follow-up emails, SMS check-ins, or satisfaction surveys automatically. By showing genuine concern and providing valuable information, you can establish yourself as a reliable resource, strengthening the client-provider relationship. Marketing automation for the win!

Feedback & Review Requests

Positive reviews and testimonials are vital for attracting new clients to your med spa. With marketing automation in place, you can send automated communications to request feedback and reviews from satisfied clients. By including links to popular review platforms or conducting customer satisfaction surveys, you can encourage clients to share their positive experiences, bolster your online reputation, and attract new clientele.

Example Welcome Email Sequence

The following welcome email sequence exemplifies what you may want to implement for your med spa. Remember to customize and tailor the content of each email to your med spa's unique offerings, brand voice, and specific welcome sequence goals.

If you'd like to download a copy of this welcome email sequence, go to https://medspamarketingbook.com/free-resources. You can make a copy and change some of the text to make it your own.

Email 1: Welcome and Introduction

Subject: Welcome to [Med Spa Name], [Client's Name]!

Hi [Client's Name],

Welcome to [Med Spa Name]! Thank you for choosing our med spa for your aesthetic needs. We're thrilled to have you as a new patient. I want to warmly welcome you and let you know what to expect during your journey with us.

At [Med Spa Name], our mission is to provide exceptional outcomes, personalized treatments, and a rejuvenating experience that leaves you feeling confident and refreshed. We offer a wide range of services, including [list key services or treatments], all delivered by our highly skilled and compassionate team of professionals.

You'll receive a few more emails from me over the next two weeks. I will share success stories of our satisfied clients, provide exclusive incentives to enhance your experience, and help guide you through your aesthetics journey with us.

If you have any immediate questions or concerns, please feel free to reply to this email, and our dedicated team will be happy to assist you. We look forward to helping you achieve your aesthetic goals.

Warm regards,

[Your Name]
[Med Spa Name]

Email 2: Tips and Preparation

Subject: Your Journey Begins: Essential Tips for a Smooth Experience

[Client's Name],

As you begin your journey with us, I want to provide you with some essential tips to ensure a smooth and enjoyable experience. Here are a few things to keep in mind as you prepare for your upcoming visit:

Arrive 15 minutes early: To maximize your time with our experts and ensure a relaxed experience, we recommend arriving 15 minutes before your appointment.

Hydration and skincare: Following your treatment, staying hydrated and maintaining a consistent skincare routine are essential. Drink plenty of water and follow any specific skincare instructions we have provided.

Clothing suggestions: Depending on the treatment you will be receiving, we recommend wearing loose, comfortable clothing. Avoid turtle necks or tight clothing on treated areas.

Avoid certain substances: Avoid alcohol or blood-thinning medications before your appointment, as they can affect the results or interfere with specific treatments.

These tips will help elevate your visit and contribute to the best possible outcomes. We are excited to have you with us and look forward to seeing you soon!

Warm regards,

[Your Name]

[Med Spa Name]

Email 3: Introducing Our Team and Expertise

Subject: Meet Our Expert Team at [Med Spa Name], [Client's Name]!

[Client's Name],

At [Med Spa Name], we pride ourselves on having a team of experienced and passionate professionals dedicated to your care and well-being. I want to take this opportunity to introduce you to a few key members of our team who will likely be supporting you throughout your journey:

[Staff Member 1]: As our lead aesthetician, [Staff Member 1] brings years of expertise in skincare and facial treatments, ensuring your skin receives the attention and care it deserves.

[Staff Member 2]: With a specialization in body contouring and non-surgical procedures, [Staff Member 2] will guide you through transformative treatments to help you achieve your desired body goals.

[Staff Member 3]: As our dedicated patient coordinator, [Staff Member 3] will be your go-to resource for any questions, scheduling needs, or concerns. They are committed to providing exceptional service and ensuring your journey with us is smooth and enjoyable.

Our team is committed to staying updated with the latest industry advancements, attending conferences, and undergoing continuous training to deliver the highest standard of care. Rest assured that you are in the hands of experts passionate about helping you look and feel your best.

We can't wait for you to meet our team in person and experience their exceptional care. Feel free to reach out if you have any questions or want to learn more about our team members.

Warm regards,

[Your Name]

[Med Spa Name]

Email 4: Success Stories and Testimonials

Subject: Real Stories, Real Results: Inspiring Testimonials from [Med Spa Name] Clients

[Client's Name],

At [Med Spa Name], we believe in the power of sharing success stories and the transformative experiences of our valued clients. I want to inspire you and reassure you that we are committed to delivering exceptional results for each of our clients.

Here are a few testimonials from clients who have achieved remarkable results through our treatments:

[Testimonial 1]: [Client Name] shares how our rejuvenating facial treatment helped her regain a youthful glow, boosting her confidence and leaving her radiant.

[Testimonial 2]: [Client Name] recounts their journey of body sculpting with us, highlighting the professionalism and expertise of our team in achieving their desired physique.

[Testimonial 3]: [Client Name] expresses their satisfaction with our personalized approach to skincare, sharing how our tailored recommendations transformed their skin health and appearance.

These testimonials represent just a fraction of the success stories we've had the privilege to be a part of. You are in good hands when you come to [Med Spa Name].

We can't wait to create your success story together. If you have any questions or would like to explore specific treatments further, please don't hesitate to contact us.

Warm regards,

[Your Name]

[Med Spa Name]

Email 5: Exclusive Welcome Offer

Subject: Welcome Gift: [Med Spa Name] Exclusive Offer for [Client's Name]

[Client's Name],

To express our gratitude for choosing [Med Spa Name] and beginning your aesthetics journey with us, we have a special welcome gift exclusively for you. As a new patient, we are delighted to offer you [describe the offer, such as a percentage discount, complimentary add-on treatment, or gift certificate].

This exclusive welcome offer is our way of saying thank you and inviting you to experience the exceptional services and care we provide. I hope it enhances your experience with us and helps you achieve your aesthetic goals.

To take advantage of this offer, simply mention or present this email during your appointment, and our team will ensure it is applied to your selected treatment.

We look forward to providing you with an exceptional experience and helping you discover the transformative possibilities at [Med Spa Name]. If you have any questions or need assistance, please contact us.

Warm regards,

[Your Name]

[Med Spa Name]

Automation & HIPAA Compliance

HIPAA compliance complicates marketing automation for medical spas. Working with a HIPAA-compliant marketing automation platform is crucial to ensure the privacy and security of your patient information and, of course, to avoid legal ramifications of non-compliance.

HIPAA sets strict regulations and standards for handling patient health information (PHI) in the healthcare industry. Medical spas are legally obligated to protect patient privacy and maintain the security of their health information. Utilizing a HIPAA-compliant marketing automation platform ensures patient data is protected and kept confidential throughout all marketing activities, including email campaigns, SMS, and automation workflows.

Not all marketing automation platforms are HIPAA compliant, so it's important to research different marketing automation platforms and carefully evaluate their HIPAA compliance. Look for platforms that specifically mention HIPAA compliance in their documentation or website.

Request a HIPAA Business Associate Agreement (BAA) from any platform you decide to work with. A BAA is a legally binding contract that outlines the responsibilities and obligations of the marketing automation platform regarding the protection of PHI. Ensure the platform is willing to sign a BAA, establishing its commitment to HIPAA compliance.

Prioritize HIPAA compliance with the marketing automation platform you choose, and your practice can confidently engage in marketing automation, knowing your patients' privacy is safeguarded and you're in good standing with HIPAA regulations.

CHAPTER 8

THE ESSENTIALS OF GOOD SEARCH ENGINE OPTIMIZATION

Level 2: Reach

- **Search Engine Optimization (SEO)**
- Optimized Content
- Google Maps Optimization
- Paid Ads
- Social Media

When we move into Level 2, we kick things off with search engine optimization (SEO). There's no other marketing tactic that's so wildly misunderstood, so I want to take a few minutes to demystify SEO and the search engines and break down the anatomy of the search engine results page (SERP). By understanding how each component works, you can formulate a strategy to maximize results for your medical spa.

Again, there are three core components of the search engine results page—paid ads, map listings, and organic results. I'll explain each element in more detail.

1. **Paid Ads/PPC Ads**: In the paid section of the search engines, you can select relevant keywords for your practice and then pay to be listed in the search results. It's referred to as PPC, which is short for "pay-per-click," because rather than paying a flat monthly or daily fee for placement, you only pay each time someone clicks on the link.

2. **Map Listings**: Google Maps listings have become very important because they are the first thing that comes up in search results for most locally-based searches. If someone searches for providers of a particular treatment in your area, chances are the map listings will be the first thing they look at. Unlike the paid section of the search engine, you can't buy your way into the map

listings; you must earn it. Once you do, there is no per-click cost associated with being in this section of the search engine.

3. **Organic Listings**: The organic listings section of the search engine results page appears directly beneath the map listings in many local searches but directly beneath the paid listings in the absence of the map listings (the map section only shows up in specific local searches). Like map listings, you can't buy your way into this section of the search engines, and there is no associated per-click cost.

Now that you understand the three major components of the search engine results page and the differences between paid listings, map listings, and organic listings, you're probably wondering which section is the most important. I'm asked this question all the time!

The fact is that all three components are important, and each should have a place in your online marketing program. By incorporating all three sections in your overall marketing plan, you can get your practice to show up as often as possible when someone searches for the medical spa treatments you provide.

With that said, assuming you are operating on a limited budget and need to make each marketing dollar count, you need to focus your investment on the sections that will drive the strongest return on investment (ROI). Research indicates that most people look directly at the map and organic listings when searching, and their eyes simply glance over the paid listings.

SEO isn't as instantaneous as PPC ads, so I highly recommend starting on your SEO as soon as possible. It will likely take a few months to get your website to appear in the organic listings, so the sooner you start, the sooner you can get that premium placement.

How Search Engines Work

It's important to understand how search engines work. This includes the process of crawling and indexing webpages, as well as the concept of page rank. Search engines work by crawling billions of web pages using their web crawlers or spiders. These web crawlers are also known as search engine bots.

Search Engine Indexing

Once a search engine discovers a web page, the page is added to a search engine data structure called an index. A search engine index includes all the crawled web URLs and several important key elements. The search engine collects data about the content of each web page, such as:

- The keywords
- Type of content
- The uniqueness of the page
- User engagement with the page

Search Engine Algorithm

A search engine algorithm is a complex set of formulas that work together to display relevant, high-quality search results that will fulfill the user's search query as quickly as possible.

When a search query is entered into the search engine by a potential user, the search engine tries to identify all the pages that are deemed relevant. During this process, the search engine uses an algorithm to instantly consider thousands of elements, such as the search query typed into the search engine, the user's location, type of device, and previous search history. The algorithm then hierarchically ranks the most relevant pages into results.

The algorithm used to rank the most relevant web pages differs for each search engine. For example, a web page that ranks at the top of the SERP for a search query in Google may not rank highly for the same query in Bing.

SEO is both an art and a science but not insurmountable. With everything you're learning from reading this book, I can practically guarantee that you are gaining skills that will serve you and your practice well.

Keyword Optimization

Keyword optimization works hand in hand with SEO, so before moving on to other marketing strategies, let's expand your SEO knowledge by diving deeper into keywords.

Getting your med spa listed in the organic section of search engines comes down to two core factors:

On-Page Optimization: Having the proper on-page optimization so Google knows what you do and the general area you serve is crucial for your practice's online visibility. On-page optimization allows Google to index your web pages for the right keywords. You do this by having pages for each of your services and then optimizing them for specific keyword combinations. For example, "botox + Seattle," "CoolSculpting + Seattle," "laser hair removal + Seattle," etc.

Off-Page Optimization: Creating enough authority and transparency so Google ranks your med spa website on page one (rather than page ten) for those specific keywords is done through off-page optimization. Ultimately, it comes down to having credible inbound links and citations from other websites to your website and individual pages. Whoever has the most credible inbound links, citations, and reviews, will be the most successful with their listing placement.

Before you start creating pages and trying to do the on-page optimization work, you need to be clear on the most commonly searched keywords relative to the services and treatments your practice offers. It's important to conduct thorough keyword research to find the optimal keywords that will help you bring in more clients. By understanding the keywords, you can optimize your website for the words that will drive qualified traffic.

How to Conduct Keyword Research

Several tools can be used to conduct keyword research. Some are free, while others have a monthly cost associated with them. Some better keyword research tools include Wordstream, Google Ads Keyword Planner, and SEMRush.

I've developed instructions based on the free Google Ads Keyword Planner. To use the tool, you'll need to:

- Develop a list of the cities near your practice's physical location (your primary city location and the smaller surrounding towns) and save it in a .txt file
- Develop a list of your services/treatments and save it in a .txt file
- Go to www.mergewords.com:
  - Paste your list of cities in column 1
  - Paste your list of services in column 2
  - Press the "Merge!" button
  - The tool will generate a list of all your services combined with your cities of service
- Go to Google.com and search "Google Keyword Planner" or go directly to https://ads.google.com/aw/keywordplaner (You'll need to log in or create an account):
  - Paste your list of merged keywords into the "word or phrase" box
  - Press "Submit"
- Your list now shows the search volume beside each keyword – Sort the list from greatest to smallest

You now have a list of keywords that people commonly search for. With this list, you can map out keywords to specific pages on your website and feel confident that you are basing your strategy on opportunity rather than a guesstimate.

Commonly Searched Med Spa Keywords

The list of keywords below contains 10 of the most popular keywords for specific treatments. Your list will look like this but should be specific to your med spa's unique service offering.

laser hair removal	450,000
botox	165,000
microneedling	165,000
hydrafacials	110,000
chemical peel	90,500
body sculpting	49,500
juvederm	40,500
dermal fillers	22,200
rf microneedling	18,100
skin tightening	14,800

Based on this data, to get the most from the internet from an SEO perspective, you will want to create content on your website for the following keyword combinations:

Your City + laser hair removal

Your City + botox

Your City + microneedling

Your City + hydrafacials

Your City + chemical peel

Your City + body sculpting

Your City + juvederm

Your City + dermal fillers

Your City + rf microneedling

Your City + skin tightening

Map Out Your Website Pages

Now that you have a list of the most commonly searched keywords for medical spas in your area, you can begin mapping out the pages which need to be added to your website. Keep in mind each page on your website can only be optimized for a few keyword combinations.

Be sure you have each keyword mapped to a specific page on your site.

Keyword	Mapped to what page
Main Keyword	Home
Keyword 1	Treatment 1
Keyword 2	Treatment 2
Keyword 3	Treatment 3
Keyword 4	Treatment 4
Keyword 5	Treatment 5

With your keyword mapping complete, you can start thinking about how to optimize each of those pages for the major search engines.

How to Optimize for Organic Search

Step 1 – Assess Your Website

I'm going to assume that you already have a website. The keyword research exercise may reveal additional pages that need to be added to your website. If this is your case, don't delay on those pages. You're missing out on potential business without them.

By having separate pages highlighting each of your services and treatments offered (combined with city modifiers), you can get listed in the search engines for each of those different keyword combinations. You also want to ensure you have all the standard pages that every med spa needs.

Using Seattle as our example city and based on the keyword research above, your page breakdown would look something like this:

First, the standard pages: Home, About, Contact, Promotions & Events.

Then, pages for each treatment you offer: Seattle Laser Hair Removal, Seattle Botox, Seattle Microneedling, Seattle Hydrafacials, and so on.

Again, if your website is missing any of these important pages, make a plan to get them added. Without those pages, you're missing an opportunity to get more leads in the door.

Step 2 – Optimize the Pages

Once the pages are all in place for each of your treatments, each page needs to be optimized from an SEO perspective to make the search engines understand what the page is about.

Here are some of the most important elements that need to be taken care of for on-page search engine optimization:

- Unique title tag on each page
- H1 tag restating the title tag on each page
- Images named with primary keywords
- URL containing page keyword
- Anchor text on each page and built into footer (Your City + Med Spa)
- XML sitemap should be created and submitted to Google Search Console and Bing Webmaster Tools

How to Build Up Website Authority

Once you've added any missing pages to your website and the on-page SEO is complete, the next step is off-page SEO. This is primarily acquiring inbound links to your website. And when I say "links," I'm referring to other websites linking to your website, which I'll explain more with specific examples.

Everything we have discussed to this point is laying the groundwork. The pages need to be in order to even be in the running. However, the number of QUALITY inbound links and web references to those pages greatly impact where your pages appear in search engine results.

Having the right pages and optimizing them is just the beginning. The only way to get your site to rank above your competition is by having more quality inbound links and citations to your site.

Again, if there is any secret sauce to ranking well in the search engines, it really is links and authority. The big challenge is that you can't just use garbage links. You don't want to have a ton of links from terrible websites, which could actually hurt your authority and rankings. You must focus on getting quality links through content creation and strategic link building. Honestly, it can be a grueling, tedious process, but it's definitely worth the effort.

Finding Quality Link Opportunities

First, look at your potential circle of linking opportunities. You want to take advantage of as many of these opportunities as possible.

1. **Association Links**: Be sure that you have a link to your website from any industry associations that you belong to (Ex. Business associations, Chamber of Commerce, Networking groups, etc.). **Directory Listings**: Get your site listed on as many directory websites as possible (Angie's List, Yahoo Local Directory, Judy's Book, Yelp.com, etc.)

2. **Create Interesting Content/Articles**: This is probably the #1 source of inbound links. For example, you can write an article about a particular service or treatment and push it out to thousands of people through article directory sites that may each contain a link back to a specific page on your site.

3. **Competitive Link Acquisition**: This is the process of using tools like SEMRush to see what links your top competitors have and then getting those same or similar links directed to your website.

Let's take a closer look at each type of link so that you understand where to start with your link-building plan.

Industry Associations

Ensure you have a link to your website from any industry associations you belong to (Ex, National industry associations, local chapters of larger associations, Chamber of Commerce, Networking groups, etc.). In the graphic, I reference some aesthetics associations.

Most associations have a published list of members, so when you are an association member, you'll have a link back to your website. Associations love to share all of the benefits of becoming a member, but this is a big benefit that never gets mentioned.

Business Directories

There are a number of "low-hanging fruit" links, which are your online directory listings. Some examples include Google Maps, Bing Places for Business, City Search, Yelp.com, Yellow Pages, and so on. All of those online listings let you display your company name, address, phone number, and a link back to your website. Some of them even allow reviews.

For the most part, adding your business information to those directories is completely free of charge. Some directories can be pretty aggressive in their sales efforts to get you to bump up to a paid account. You do NOT need a paid listing to get the effect you want from the listing.

Links are also valuable for your Google Maps optimization because they give you citations which are very important for getting ranked on the map. Just remember that your NAP (Name, Address, Phone) must be the same everywhere online.

A great way to find additional online directories to add your med spa to would be to search in Google for "med spa business directory." This should produce a great list of potential directory sites to add your practice to. There are also tools for this, like BrightLocal or White Spark, that can provide you with a list of good directory sources.

Non-Competitive Affiliated Industries & Local Businesses

One effective strategy for acquiring valuable backlinks is establishing partnerships with non-competitive affiliated industries and local businesses.

Non-competitive affiliated industries have some connection to your business but do not directly compete with your services. Look for complementary industries that share a similar target audience with you. The key is to find relevant businesses and add value to the same customer base without being competitors.

By partnering with non-competing businesses, you can exchange backlinks or create content collaborations that link to each other's websites. These backlinks are highly valuable in demonstrating the credibility and authority of your website to search engines like Google. These partnerships can also offer valuable opportunities like co-hosting events, cross promotions, and even sharing physical space.

For med spas, potential partnerships can be found with businesses such as cosmetic dentists, gyms, or wedding photographers. Get curious and think about all the different industries and businesses serving your potential clients right now.

Supplier Websites

One often overlooked source of potential backlinks is the websites of your suppliers or vendors. Leveraging supplier websites for link building presents a valuable opportunity to strengthen your website's authority, relevance, and credibility within your industry.

Look at your list of suppliers, from your equipment to the skincare products you sell and products you use and order regularly. Many supplier websites have a section dedicated to listing their resellers or partners, showcasing businesses that distribute their products or utilize their services.

Supplier websites often carry a certain level of authority and credibility within your industry. When they link to your website as one of their trusted resellers or partners, it can positively influence search engines' perception of your site. The links act as trust signals to both search engines and potential clients, indicating that your business is associated with well-established and trustworthy entities within the industry.

Social Media Profiles

Another "low-hanging fruit" linking opportunity is social media profiles. There's an entire chapter later in this book about the power of social media. For now, simply ensure each profile links to your website.

From a link-building perspective alone, you should have social media profiles for your practice on Instagram, Facebook, TikTok, Twitter, LinkedIn, Pinterest, and YouTube. They will allow you to enter your company's name, address, phone number, business description, and a link to your website.

I know Linktree and similar tools have been popular for businesses on Instagram. If that's your only option, keep doing it! However, if you can add a similar page to your website instead, that would be better so that you're linking to your own website rather than a 3rd party tool.

Local Associations

Don't forget to consider the local associations that you're involved in. If you're a member of your local Chamber of Commerce, a networking group like BNI (Business Networking International), or if you're involved with a local charity, find out if they list their members or donors on their websites.

You can also find local associations by searching for "your city business directory." This should give you a list of potential local directory sites to add your practice to. Again, make sure you're only connecting with quality websites. Don't make the mistake of thinking all "local" sites are run by people in your community. Consider them just as carefully as you do any others.

Competitive Link Acquisition

Competitive link acquisition is figuring out who is in the top position for your most important keywords, reverse engineering their link profile to see their links, and getting the same or similar links pointing back to your website.

A simple way to do this is just to go to Google and type in "your city + your service" and see which med spas are in the top few positions. Once you identify the med spa in the #1 position, you can use tools like SEMRush, or Majestic SEO to get a list of websites linking to your competitor.

Then visit each linking website to determine how to get a link from that website too. By analyzing the types of links they have, you can systematically mimic those links and get them directed to your website as well. Don't just do this for your first competitor but also for your second, third, fourth, and fifth competitors.

If you build out your site for your services and treatments, optimize the pages using SEO best practices and then systematically obtain inbound links consistently, you will start to move up the ranks in the search engines for your most important keywords.

CHAPTER 9

ESTABLISHING YOUR MEDSPA'S AUTHORITY & TRUST WITH CONTENT

Level 2: Reach

- Search Engine Optimization (SEO)
- **Optimized Content**
- Google Maps Optimization
- Paid Ads
- Social Media

The Importance of Optimizing Your Content

Google loves fresh content! In some cases, with changes in the algorithm, your website can lose ground in the search engine results if there isn't consistent new content on your website. This can happen even if you've got a great website with the correct title tags and all the best links.

Regularly adding new content to your website is crucial to a successful SEO strategy. It can help improve your visibility in search engine results, drive more traffic, and establish your site as an authority in your field.

Understanding Website Content

How does it actually work? It's important, you get that, but how does it work? Let's break it down into the most important ways new content helps your website.

Updated Indexing: Search engines like Google favor fresh, updated content. When you regularly update your website with new content, search engines will crawl and index your site more frequently, improving your visibility in search results.

Keyword Opportunities: Each new piece of content is an opportunity to target a specific keyword related to your practice. The more quality content you have, the more chances you have to rank for different keywords.

User Engagement: Fresh content can keep your audience engaged, encouraging them to spend more time on your site and interact with your content. This can lead to lower bounce rates and higher user engagement, positively impacting your SEO.

Authority and Expertise: Regularly publishing high-quality content can establish your site as an authority in your field. This can increase your site's trustworthiness and relevance, which search engines consider when ranking sites.

Backlink Opportunities: Quality content can earn you backlinks from other websites. Backlinks are a significant factor in how search engines rank websites. The more high-quality backlinks you have, the better your site will perform in search engine results.

Social Sharing: New, engaging content is more likely to be shared on social media. This can increase your visibility, drive more traffic to your site, and improve your search engine rankings.

Long-Tail Search Queries: New content allows you to target long-tail queries, which are often less competitive and can drive highly targeted traffic to your site. These are specific phrases that users search for, and they can be easier to rank for than more common keywords.

Developing a Content Strategy

It is important to have a system where you create and post content on your website regularly. I want to give you a framework for determining what kind of content you could produce and how to do it consistently.

Types of Content

Remember that content doesn't have to be just written words. Blog posts are typically the first people think of when discussing content, but content comes in various forms. Depending on the purpose and goals of your content, it can be short-form videos, blog posts, webinars, ebooks, photos, audio files, and so on!

Give some thought to what content creation method works best for **you**. Some people are great writers, and that's their strength. Other people like to be on camera. And sometimes what works best for you evolves over time or in different seasons of life and business. As long as you create content, *how* you do it can be a fluid decision.

Because video is so popular and versatile, I'll use it as an example. First, a quick note about the quality of the videos you create. If you've put off doing video because you think it will require a professional camera and a whole production crew, think again! You may be surprised to learn that less polished videos perform better online. So pull out your iPhone, and you have the essential equipment for creating videos.

Back to the example – A med spa director, aesthetician, or injector can record themselves explaining a treatment the practice offers in the same manner they would explain it to a patient. That video can easily be turned into multiple pieces of content.

You'll have a video, which can be uploaded to YouTube, Vimeo, etc. This one piece of content can create multiple invaluable links to your website. Plus, the video can be cut up into smaller segments to use on your social media channels. You can save the audio portion of the video, and you've got an audio file for your website and other various sites. You can have the video transcribed, and now you have content for a new blog post.

Repurpose your content in as many ways as possible to truly take advantage of the value of your content.

Subject-Matter Experts

First, you must understand that you are already a subject matter expert. You might not consider yourself a writer or a content creator, but there's no doubt that you are a subject matter expert.

You know countless things related to medical spa services that the general population does not. You're an expert and likely have a team of aesthetics professionals who are also experts. A team of experts makes content creation much more manageable for everyone.

You may not think it at first, but there are a ton of aesthetics topics that you can create content about. In most cases, it's simply a matter of making the time to brainstorm and generate a list of topic ideas.

Content Consistency

You want to create content consistently, using the blog on your website as the hub to post it but then syndicate it to various sources. You can syndicate it to article directory sites if it's in text form and send it to video sites like YouTube and Vimeo if it's in video form. Doing this keeps the content fresh on your website and creates a lot of authority, which will help with the overall ranking of your website on search engines.

It's important to appropriate each link-building opportunity to maximize your area's rank potential. Medical spa services are highly competitive from an SEO perspective. Many practices want to rank for the exact keywords, and many of them have invested heavily in online marketing and getting themselves higher in the search engines. Of course, the more medical spas in your local area, the more competitive this gets.

Your Content Creation Calendar

Now that you know the types of content you'll create, you'll want to create a content creation calendar. This will help you plan your content creation and publishing the content in advance.

This calendar can be as simple or complex as you need it to be. Whether you want a basic list of topics and format or a detailed spreadsheet that includes dates, statuses, channels, etc., is totally up to you. Your content creatio calendar is your med spa's guide to ensure the content aligns with your overall goals and marketing strategy and that you publish content regularly.

Optimized Website Content

Creating content is an invaluable part of an ongoing process for businesses. But content that isn't optimized is a tremendous lost opportunity for businesses. Optimizing your content is a crucial step in the process.

Your content should address the needs and interests of your target audience and provide them with helpful information. This content should be created using keywords identified in your keyword research. Incorporate these keywords and phrases strategically into your content to improve its visibility in search engine results.

Every published blog post should be considered incomplete until optimized. This includes a compelling title tag and meta description, which is what shows up on the search engine results page.

In the blog post, you'll want to include keywords in your headings and URL. Tools such as SurferSEO will grade your content to let you know if it's optimized well for SEO. This also includes internal linking and content that is well-structured, easy to read, and properly formatted.

Building a solid network of high-quality backlinks from reputable websites is integral to SEO but not always feasible for every blog post. Backlinks are an essential ranking factor, so with blog posts, focus on earning links naturally through compelling content that people want to share. Your part of this process is to promote your content through various channels to improve its chances of attracting organic traffic and backlinks.

Remember, optimizing your content for SEO is an ongoing process. It requires consistency, continuous improvement, and up-to-date industry trends and search engine algorithm changes.

Each piece of content you publish contributes to your overall goals, whether increasing website traffic, boosting engagement rates, or driving sales. Later in this book, I'll cover tracking and measuring your content. Tracking when and where each content is published allows you to draw correlations between your content efforts and performance metrics. It transforms your content strategy into a powerful instrument for strategic decision-making.

Now that you've built your website, optimized it correctly, and got an ongoing link-building and content development strategy, you want to start looking at Google Maps optimization and getting ranked in Google Maps.

CHAPTER 10

HOW TO GET RANKED IN GOOGLE MAPS

Level 2: Reach

- Search Engine Optimization (SEO)
- Optimized Content
- **Google Maps Optimization**
- Paid Ads
- Social Media

The Fundamentals of Google Maps Ranking

Getting listed on the first page of Google Maps for "Your City + Service" comes down to four primary factors:

- A claimed and verified Google Maps listing
- An optimized Google Business Profile for the area your medical spa is located in

- A consistent NAP (Name, Address, Phone Number) profile across the web so that Google feels confident that you are a legitimate organization located in the place you have listed and serving the market you claim to serve
- Reviews from your clients in your region

If you have these four factors working in your favor, you will significantly improve the probability of ranking on page one of Google Maps in your market.

Establish Your Med Spa's NAP

As I mentioned above, having a consistent name, address, and phone number for your med spa across the web is essential for ranking well on Google Maps in your area. Google sees your business entity listed with the exact details throughout the internet and considers each entity listing as a signal of authority.

So rather than jumping directly into claiming your Google Maps listing and building citations, it's critical that you start by determining your true NAP so that you can ensure it's referenced consistently across the web.

When I say to make sure it's consistent, I mean down to the character. If your med spa's name is "Radiant & Rejuvenation MedSpa," it must always be shown that exact way online. It can't be "Radiant and Rejuvenation MedSpa," "Radiant & Rejuvenation Spa," or "Radiant & Rejuv. MedSpa" in different places on the web.

Similarly, if your med spa's location has a suite number, you don't want to change how you write "suite" throughout the web. You must decide if it will always be written out as "suite" or shortened to "ste." Or perhaps you want to consider it a "unit" or "#." And if your street address includes "SW," you don't want to add it as "Southwest" anywhere online.

These inconsistencies will thwart your efforts. So ensure you've decided on your *exact* NAP and then stick to it as you list your company details in various directory sources.

There is one small caveat with your phone number. When creating citations, or directory listings, for your practice, you want to use your primary business phone number. However, your "primary" business number will be added as a secondary phone number in your Google Maps listing. Your "primary" phone number in the listing should be a tracking number. This is important to monitor your Google Maps results.

A good way to determine what Google considers your NAP is to search for "Your Medspa" on Google and see what is referenced on Google Maps. See how that compares to other high-authority sites like YP.com, Yelp.com, and others. Look for the predominant combination of NAP and reference for all your directory work going forward.

Claim Your Google Business Profile

Below is a step-by-step guide for checking, claiming, adding, and managing your Google Business Profile.

1. Go to https://www.google.com/business/.

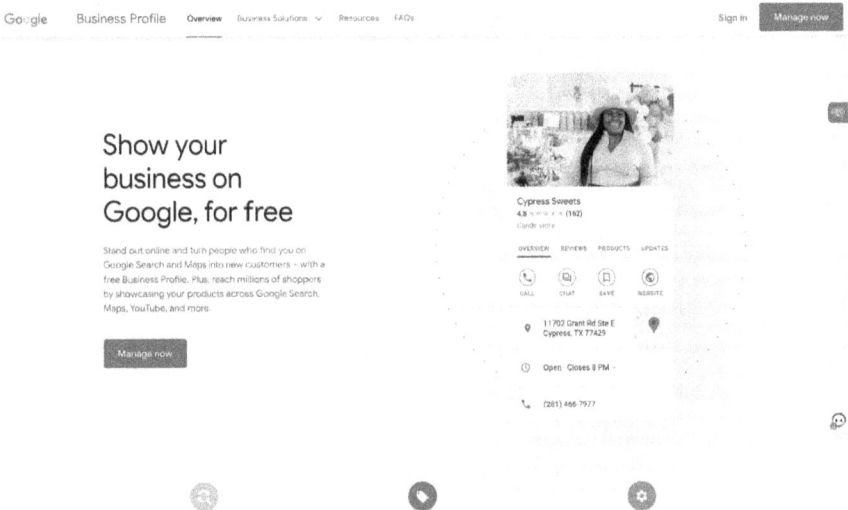

2. Create an account and claim or add your business.

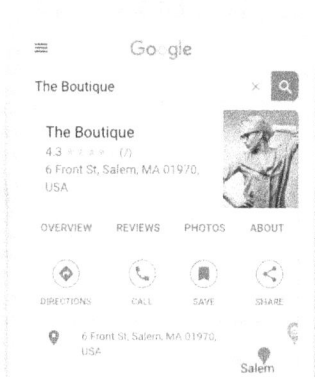

Find and manage your business

Q Type your business name

Can't find your business?

Add your business to Google

3. If you're adding your business, add your name (Don't add any additional keywords here!) and your primary category (Medical Spa).

Start building your Business Profile

This will help you get discovered by customers on Google Search and Maps

Business name*

Business category*

You can change this and more later

By continuing, you're agreeing to these Terms of Service and Privacy Policy

Next

4. Answer each question and provide all pertinent information.

5. Select a verification method (Google's options vary on a case-by-case basis).

While waiting for your business to be verified, you can still optimize your profile. The changes just won't be published until the verification process is complete.

Optimize Your Google Business Profile

You'll manage your Google Maps listing from your Google Business Profile (GBP). This is where you'll make changes to your company information, share information about your services, and gain insights into the performance of your listing, which includes the keywords users searched for to see your profile and the number of phone calls, website clicks, and directions to your location.

Google Business Profile Best Practices

Company Name: Always use your legal business name—don't try to cram additional words into the name field. For example, if your practice's name is "Rejuvenation Medspa," don't try adding keywords like "Rejuvenation Medspa - Dallas." This is against Google's terms of service and can reduce your probability of ranking. Even worse, it can get your profile suspended.

Address: Refer to the true NAP you established earlier in this chapter. Add your address exactly as you recorded it. Again, this is very important because you will use the same address in all the other online directory listings like YellowPages.com, CitySearch.com, Yelp.com, etc.

Phone Number: Use a local number and not an 800 number. Eight hundred numbers tend not to rank as well. If you aren't using a tracking number, your phone number can go into the primary phone number field. If you are using a tracking number, add the tracking number in the primary phone number field and your actual phone number in the secondary phone number field.

Business Categories: Google has a set list of business categories that you need to choose from. As you begin to type into the category fields, options will come up for you. Your primary business category will likely be "Medical spa," but for some readers, it might be "Plastic surgeon," "Plastic surgery clinic," or "Dermatologist." A few other business categories to consider are:

Skin care clinic   Laser hair removal service
Facial spa   Wellness center
Weight loss service   Medical office
Hair removal service

Photos & Videos: Use this opportunity to upload authentic content about your practice. Using real images of your team, office, and equipment is always best rather than stock photos here. Even better, use photos taken with a cell phone so that the pictures are already geotagged for your location. The images and videos don't have to be professionally produced; they'll resonate better with people if they aren't.

You can get more juice from this section by saving the images with a naming convention like "your city + medical spa - your company name" rather than the standard file name. I recommend uploading the following types of photos:

- Logo
- Cover photo
- Location exterior (5)
- Location interior (5)
- Team (5)

Products & Services: You can add your services or treatments in two places in your Google Business Profile. The first place is in the services area. Be sure to include complete descriptions for each service, as these are now shown to searchers in your profile. You always want to add your treatments as "products." In this section, you'll include a description and a photo.

Business Details: You want to complete your profile as thoroughly as possible. This includes adding a well-written business description, your business hours, and answering yes or no to several details related to accessibility, accepted payment types, how you identify as the owner, and if appointments are required. Again, be thorough so that your profile is as complete as possible.

Duplicate Listings

Once you have optimized your listing using the best practices referenced above, you want to ensure you don't have duplicate listings on Google Maps. We have found that even just one or two duplicates can prevent your listing from ranking on page one. Search for "Company Name, City" in Google to identify and merge duplicate listings.

To clean up duplicates, click on the listing in question and "Suggest an edit." You'll then have the option to click on "Change name or other details," which is where you'd suggest a change to the listing's name, location, hours, etc., or "Close or remove," which is where you can mark a business closed, non-existent, or a duplicate. Once you click "Close or remove," you'll see several options, including "Duplicate of another place."

Develop Authority for Your Google Maps Listing

Now that you have claimed your GBP and optimized it to its fullest, you must build authority. Unfortunately, having a claimed and well-optimized local listing doesn't automatically rank your business on page one.

Google wants to list the most legitimate and qualified providers first.

There are several ranking factors that Google, or any other search engine, considers to determine a company's legitimacy. One of the factors is how widely the business or "entity," as Google calls it, is referenced on various online directory sites such as Yellow Pages, City Search, and Yelp.

Citations

Citations, also called business listings or directory listings, are web references to your company as an entity. We often look at the links flowing toward a company's website online, but with citations, our focus is on the entity, which is why it's so vital that you're always using your established NAP.

You can claim your listings manually as you've done with your GBP or use a directory submission service. Submission services are great because they handle several citations for you. A few popular submission services are Yext, BrightLocal, and Moz Local.

I prefer to claim the most valuable or impactful listings, ensuring I am in control and can make updates or edits as needed. Then I use a submission service to submit business details to aggregators and a handful of high-value directories but not quite as valuable as the sources listed below.

TOP Citation Sources to Claim Manually:

- Google Maps
- Apple Maps
- Bing Places for Business
- Yelp
- High-value directories like RealSelf

Online Reviews

You've established your true NAP, claimed and optimized your GBP, and developed your citations across the web. The next step is obtaining reviews. Online reviews are a critical aspect of your medical spa's online presence. Reviews are so essential I've devoted an entire chapter to them. Since we've already covered online reviews, I'll keep it brief here.

First, you should never attempt to game the system with fake or fraudulent reviews. They aren't going to help you. You need genuine reviews from your actual clients. Google pays close attention to the reviewer's profile.

If someone is an active Google user with a Gmail account, a YouTube channel, and potentially a Local Guide status, that's all connected to a Google profile. Say that person with the active profile has had their account for seven years and is near your location. If she writes a review for your practice, it would be considered credible and will count in your favor.

Alternatively, suppose someone creates a Gmail right before writing a review. In that case, they have no other Google accounts tied to their Gmail, and no history is associated with the profile. Google gives that review very little weight. It's obviously not credible to Google, and there's a good chance that Google will flag the review as a fraudulent submission.

It is important to have an authentic strategy when connecting with real people who will write genuine reviews. Again, don't try to game the system. Google is fully aware of these attempts, and so is Yelp and several other popular online review sites.

Don't Neglect Email Addresses

To execute a scaleable strategy to increase the number of positive reviews of your practice, you'll need your clients' email addresses. The best time to ask for an email address is when your client is booking a treatment.

If you wait until after the treatment when your patient is checking out, your front desk staff will run into more resistance. However, suppose you collect an email address when someone is scheduling an appointment. In that case, they are far less resistant because they're already providing other information to get the desired outcome—an appointment at your med spa. It's just a difference in mindset.

The number of reviews you have from actual clients will increase exponentially if you utilize marketing automation (emails and SMS messages) to request reviews from happy clients. Because reviews and citations work harmoniously for ranking, this is how you'll start seeing improved online performance.

Follow these steps to properly claim your Google Maps listing, develop your authority with quality citations, and put a systematic process in place to get genuine reviews from your clients. You will be well on your way to dominating Google Maps in your market.

CHAPTER 11

REACHING A WIDER AUDIENCE WITH PAID ADS

Level 2: Reach

- Search Engine Optimization (SEO)
- Optimized Content
- Google Maps Optimization
- **Paid Ads**
- Social Media

Let's revisit the digital marketing plan referenced in chapter four of this book. You will recall that your digital marketing plan's foundation should be organic, non-paid marketing efforts (website, SEO, Google Maps, social media marketing, video marketing, etc.). Once you have a strong foundation, you'll be ready to invest in paid online marketing initiatives.

In this chapter, we will talk about pay-per-click (PPC) marketing to help you understand how it works, why it should be integrated into your overall marketing strategy, and how you can run an effective program to drive leads and sales for your practice.

Introduction to PPC Advertising

PPC marketing is an integral part of a digital marketing plan for medical spas because it allows your practice to reach your target audience with relevant ads when actively searching for your services.

Let's review how Google Ads works. - In the simplest sense, you pay on a per-click basis and can choose your keywords (Example: medical spa, your city medical spa, your city med spa, medspa). As you pick those words, you bid and pay on a per-click basis.

So, let's say you're bidding on the keywords "San Antonio med spa," and there are a lot of other med spas in that city that want to rank for that keyword. If you say that you'll pay $2/click and your competitor says they'll pay $5/click, they will be at the top. Assuming nobody else has placed a higher bid, $2 will be ranked second; if the next highest bid is $1.20, that will follow.

With that foundational understanding of how the auction system works, I'll explain why it isn't 100% the reality. What tends to happen is that pay-per-click campaigns are often built on the notion that the highest bid wins. So, businesses pick their keywords, throw up the highest bid per click, and hope everything turns out how they want it.

You are bidding against your competitors to determine how you will rank for your keywords, and it involves more than just the bid amount. I'll explain this later in this chapter when we examine why many PPC campaigns fail.

Benefits of Pay-Per-Click Campaigns

In my opinion, the following benefits of PPC marketing are a few of the best reasons to incorporate it into your digital marketing plan:

- Show up in search engine results quickly

- Show up as often as possible where potential clients are looking

- Show up for non-geo-modified terms that are related to your treatments

- Mobile searches

Now, let's look at those benefits in greater detail.

Fast Visibility

Unlike an SEO program, PPC gets things happening relatively quickly. An SEO program requires setting up your website, building links, and having the proper on-page optimization. This process can take some time to materialize. What you do today and tomorrow will pay dividends for your practice in three to four months.

With PPC advertising, you set up your campaign and should start to see your ads serve in just a few days. It can drive good traffic for your med spa, especially during important times when you must be highly visible online.

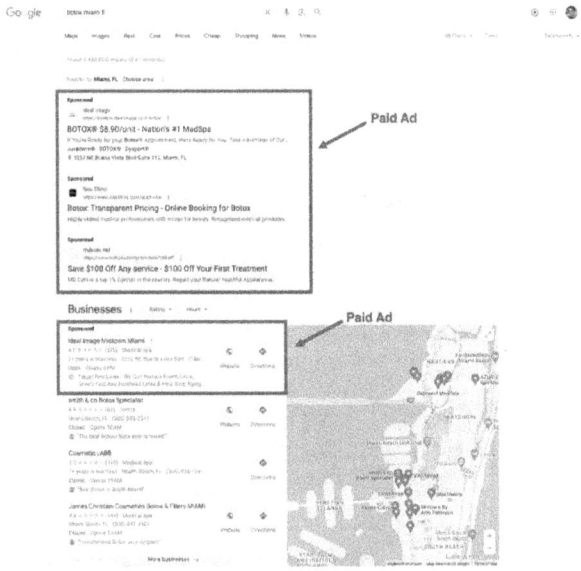

The Right Place at the Right Time

You want to show up as often as possible when someone's looking for your treatments. A PPC ad that appears at the top, on the map, and in the organic section is essential.

Now you've got the opportunity to show up in multiple places and significantly improve the chances of getting your ad clicked on, as opposed to your competition. A PPC campaign gives you that additional position on the first page of search engine results.

An important factor of PPC marketing is that you're showing up in front of people actively looking for your services. Your ad is showing up in the right place and at the right time. People searching online will see ads. It's just a matter of whose ads they'll see, yours or your competitors.

Additional Keywords

PPC advertising also allows you to show up for keywords that you won't show up for in your organic SEO efforts. This is what we call non-geo-modified keywords.

SEO and our whole organic strategy allow us to appear in search engines when someone searches for your city + service, for example, "Portland + microneedling." That search term includes a geo-modifier (your city).

With a PPC campaign, you can show up for non-geo-modified search terms, for example, microneedling, laser hair removal, etc. By using a radius in your ad settings, you can ensure your ads only show up for people within a limited distance of your medical spa's location, eliminating the need to use a geo-modifier in the search terms.

That means if your med spa is located in Portland and someone in that area searches for "microneedling" or "laser hair removal," you can set it so that it only shows your ad to those searching within that area. Google can isolate who ran the search and where they ran it from and seamlessly show the advertisers set up for that area.

Mobile Searches

Another reason that you should consider running a PPC campaign is that you can run mobile PPC campaigns.

When someone searches for your services from a mobile device, they typically want the treatment relatively quickly. Mobile searches often have higher intent than desktop searches. People are not as apt to browse multiple pages or listings on a mobile device.

If you have a PPC campaign set up, that person searching can see your ad at the top of the page. They can simply tap your ad and automatically call your practice rather than browsing your website and researching. With mobile PPC campaigns, you pay per phone call instead of per click or lead.

PPC marketing is very powerful. If it's not included in your current marketing plan, I strongly encourage you to take another look at PPC advertising. It's an integral part of a successful digital marketing plan.

Pay-Per-Click Networks

PPC networks, such as Google Ads and Microsoft Ads, dominate the world of pay-per-click advertising across major search engines.

Google Ads, a powerhouse platform, offers extensive reach and user-friendly features. It allows advertisers to create captivating ads that appear alongside relevant search results, targeting specific demographics and locations for maximum impact.

Microsoft Ads provides an alternative audience segment and expands advertising reach.

Both networks offer powerful tools and analytics to optimize campaigns, including performance metrics and precise targeting options.

Leveraging these PPC networks empowers businesses to expand their reach, drive targeted traffic, and generate leads.

Google and Microsoft both have their networks behind them. When you work with Google's network, you gain access to YouTube, Blogger, Gmail, and around two million other websites. And when you get on the Microsoft network, you get access to Bing, Netflix, Xbox, Outlook, and many more.

Google is clearly the dominant player with no serious competition. More than 80 percent of all searches happen on Google.com. If you had to choose between Google and Microsoft, you would obviously want to use Google. However, if you can go with both, you get an additional 20% by tapping into the Microsoft network.

Additional networks are available for advertising, but those two comprise most of the search market. Running a pay-per-click campaign with both Google Ads and Microsoft Ads will allow your med spa to show up in the primary search engines that someone might be using.

Why Most PPC Campaigns Fail

While PPC marketing is a great way to get noticed, it's true that most campaigns fail. I'll explain what people do wrong and then show you how to do it right so that your campaign is successful.

Most Common PPC Mistakes

This is a short list of the most common mistakes I see:

- Setting up only ONE ad group for all services
- Not using specific text ads and landing pages for groups of keywords
- No strong call to action or OFFER on the landing page

Typically, businesses set up only one ad group for all services. So they'll include everything, like medical spa, microneedling, injectables, IPL, laser hair removal, etc., in one ad group rather than different ad groups for each type of service.

You're missing out if you're not leveraging specific text in ads and landing pages. You wind up with the same landing page and text ad, whether someone typed in "medical spa, microneedling, injectables, IPL, laser hair removal, etc." in the search engine.

Whatever was typed into the search engine was likely very specific and should match up to a very specific page. Everything is diluted when you're not using specific text ads and landing pages. With this strategy, not only will your campaign convert poorly, but your cost per click will be higher. I will explain why later in this chapter.

The other reason why most pay-per-click campaigns fail is because there isn't a strong call to action on the landing page. So, you were just charged $9 or $20 to get a potential customer to your website, and the page isn't even compelling because it doesn't have a solid call to action. It doesn't tell the consumer what to do next.

If you factor in these common reasons that PPC campaigns tend to fail, you can avoid these mistakes and set yourself up for success in executing your pay-per-click marketing.

Relevancy & Quality Scores

Let's circle back to the Google Ads auction process. Again, it's more complex than the highest bidder winning. It's much more complicated than that.

In reality, Google needs to feature the most relevant results because its endgame is to keep people using its search engine over the competition. This is how they can keep their traffic up. Google can keep its usage up and maintain that 80% market share. Plus, they can run Google Ads and make billions of dollars yearly. Ultimately, it all comes down to relevancy.

The second Google sacrifices relevancy for dollars is the second they start to lose its market share. So, Google had to figure out how to make their pay-per-click program grow around relevancy. That's why they established the quality score. They need to ensure that the person or company with more relevancy gets a higher quality score and, as a result, can have a lower cost per click.

I'll explain how this all works with an example:

If I go to Google and type in "BMW," I am obviously looking for a BMW dealer or information about BMW.

Mercedes could say, "That's our demographic too. If someone types in BMW, they're looking for a high-end vehicle. They are probably in the market to buy. Let's bid on the word BMW."

Of course, they can bid on the word. However, the person that searched for BMW isn't looking for Mercedes. So, Mercedes could say, "We'll pay $25 for every click on our ad when they search for "BMW."

But BMW might say, "That's our brand. We will compete for it, but we won't spend $25 for every click on our brand. We'll pay $1 for every click."

Based on the quality score, Google may decide to serve BMW because it's in the best interest of the person searching for the brand, the consumer. It's also in the best interest of overall relevancy. That's how the quality score works.

Three core components really drive quality score:

- Click-through rate
- Relevancy
- Quality of the landing page

As someone searches and your ad shows up on the search results page in the sponsored section, Google is tracking what percentage of those people saw your ad and clicked on it.

That's one of the primary metrics that Google analyzes. So, if your ad is relevant, speaks to the person's needs, and is compelling enough to make them click on it, Google sees this as evidence that your ad meets the searcher's needs. Google then increases your quality score because you've got a better click-through rate.

Relevancy is a significant factor here. It comes down to how relevant your ad is to the specific keyword that was typed in.

Example: If the searcher types in "laser hair removal," and your text ad reads: "We're the best medspa in the Dallas area," versus "We're the best medspa in the Dallas area, and we offer high-quality laser hair removal," which do you think is more relevant to the consumer?

Google wants the search results to be as applicable as possible. Again, they're looking at your click-through rate, the relevancy of the text ad to your keywords, and the quality of your landing page.

If your landing page (the page that you drive people to) doesn't match up with what the person just clicked on, or if it doesn't have a solid call to action, this typically causes the person to back out to go back to the search engine results. That signals to Google that you were not very relevant, and it reduces your quality score.

You can bid lower and still achieve the top position with a higher quality score. This is how you can win in the PPC marketing game because a high-quality score gets you a lower cost per click, even for the top positions.

Again, if we look at the reasons most PPC campaigns fail, we can see they're all interconnected:

- Setting up one ad group for all of your services
- Not using specific text in your ad that compels someone to click
- Not having a strong call to action on the landing page that matches up with what the consumer was looking for

All of these things lower your click-through rate and decrease relevancy. That results in a lower quality score, meaning you'll pay more per click. PPC marketing is highly competitive. If you're paying more per click, you'll eat up your ad budget without getting a reasonable return.

The visual representation of this would be setting up one Google Ads campaign for each of your services (laser hair removal, microneedling, dermal fillers, skin tightening, etc.) and having everyone land on your home page.

That is a recipe for disaster and precisely what you don't want to do. Now let's get into what you *should* do instead.

Creating Effective Ad Campaigns

Three essential steps are the foundation of creating successful PPC campaigns:

- Select your keywords for specific ad groups
- Write clear and concise ad text that's based on the keywords
- Drive searchers to a conversion-focused landing page

Ad Groups

For medical spas, there are some primary ad groups that you'll want to set up.

You need a standard med spa ad group for the general "I need a medspa" or "I'm looking for medical spa services" search. The searcher didn't get very specific, so you'll want to have a general ad group to catch those basic med spa searches.

After that, your ad groups will be based on the specific services your practice offers. For example, if you offer dermal filler, you'll want to have an ad group for people who search for "dermal filler," "dermal filler services," "dermal filler treatment," "dermal filler injections," etc. You want to group those keywords and have information available for those searches.

We could go deeper than this, but you should have an idea of what specific types of ad groups you need to set up based on the services you offer.

Ad Text

Your ad text must align perfectly with your targeted keywords for a successful ad campaign. If the keywords and ad text aren't aligned, your ad won't appear for the right people. And if it did, it wouldn't be successful. Write an ad text that genuinely speaks to that group of keywords.

As you write the ad text, it's important to use the keywords in a natural and informative way. You don't want to cram keywords into your ad text, as this will make your ad look spammy. Instead, use the keywords in a way that makes sense and helps people understand that you offer the exact service they're searching for.

Lastly, make sure your ad text is clear and concise. People should be able to understand what your ad is about at a glance. People won't click on your ad text if it is too long or complicated. Concise text is critical.

Landing Pages

How well a landing page converts visitors determines the page's quality. That starts with the keywords and ad text because those are what the landing page is built around. But there are factors in the landing page alone that need to be considered.

Ensure the content on your landing page is easy to read and makes it very clear that the searcher has found the solution they are looking for. You can accomplish this with a succinct headline and text that mirrors and expands on what the ad says, ideally with a special offer.

The page should be built with high-quality visuals. They help break up the text on the page, make it more visually appealing, and help explain the benefits of your services.

Last but not least, you must have a strong, compelling call to action shown prominently on the page. I know sometimes businesses don't want to appear too salesy online, but it needs to be clear what action the person needs to take to buy. If that isn't apparent within seconds, the searcher is more likely to move beyond your page and keep looking around.

I have a wireframe to share with you. If you'd like to download a copy of a conversion-focused template we use for landing pages, go to https://medspamarketingbook.com/free-resources.

PPC Lead Generation for Longer Sales Cycles

In some cases, cosmetic treatments have longer sales cycles, so potential patients may not pick up the phone to call your medical spa at that moment. They may be in the research phase. You can use PPC ads to capture attention during their search.

You would offer something that helps them further research the treatment they're interested in. This could be a comprehensive guide to CoolSculpting® or how to finance medical spa treatments. A guide allows you to position yourself as an authority on the topic and educate the readers in a way that will make them want to utilize your services.

Have a lead capture form on the landing page so the searcher can enter their name and email address to download the lead magnet. Then send them a well-crafted guide that educates them and sets the buying criteria in your favor. Plus, it gives you the added advantage of having the person on your email list, which allows you to send them emails that showcase your authority in the field and stay top-of-mind over time.

Catching someone early in the consideration process can work in your favor. It might be six months before they decide to invest in cosmetic treatment. But if you send them one email a week, when they become ready to move forward, you've made the decision easy for them. They've already seen you in their inbox several times, and you've added so much value that choosing your medical spa is a no-brainer for them.

This is an incredibly effective way to position you and your med spa for longer sales cycles. This strategy ensures your lead generation efforts are working on autopilot to convert more leads into patients now and later.

Google Ads Best Practices

We've gone over the core components of successful PPC campaigns. Now, we'll look at some essential best practices to ensure your campaigns will help you reach your business goals.

Google Ads Assets

Google Ads assets (previously called extensions) are additional information that can be added to your ad, such as your phone number, address, or website links. Ad assets can help to make your ads more visible and informative, and they can also help to improve your click-through rate.

In Chapter ten, I explained how to set up your Google Maps listing and optimize it to rank in Google Maps. You want to use the same Gmail account for both claiming your maps listing and with Google Ads so that you can access assets and add your business location and a direct link to your Google Business Profile.

Including additional assets to your ads helps make your ads stand out to attract more attention than the other ads. It also makes it easier for someone to click on your ad and quickly get helpful information that will help them decide to take action to schedule with you.

Split Testing

Split testing is a critical best practice for running ads. Split testing means you have multiple ads for every one of your ad groups. That way, you can split test the ads to see how they perform and determine which converts best.

For example, check out the ad performance below for a steak restaurant. Each ad is simply a different variation of the same messaging. They're both going to get an equal share. If there are 1,000 impressions, you could distribute 500 impressions to each one.

By split testing the ads, you can determine which one had a higher click-through rate. Then you can drop the lowest-performing ad and create a new one. At the end of the month, you can compare those two ads and see which one performed better. And so the process goes—split testing to continuously improve your click-through ratios.

Remember, having better click-through rates will get traffic to your landing page and give you a better quality score. This will eventually reduce your cost per click, making it more profitable for your medical spa over time.

Exact Match & Negative Keywords

You always want to use exact match rather than broad match. If you choose broad match, you can find your ads showing up on the search engines for many keywords that have nothing to do with your medical spa services.

The other thing you want to do is pay attention to negative keywords, which are keywords you don't want to appear for in the search engine.

A great example of this is "jobs," "employment," "marketing," etc.

If someone types in "your city medspa," that's great. If they type in "your city medspa jobs," that's somebody looking for employment at a med spa. Unless you are trying to fill a position or if you actually want to use your pay-per-click budget to get applicants, it's probably not the kind of person you want to attract.

Setting up negative keywords means, for example, if someone types in "jobs," "employment," or "marketing" anywhere in their search, it blocks your ads from those search results. By removing your ads from irrelevant searches, you won't pay for clicks that don't support your objective.

Mobile Search vs. Desktop Search

I talked about ensuring you've set up mobile pay-per-click campaigns. I've mentioned the significant transition between people searching on their mobile devices and people searching on their computers.

These days, most web visits are conducted on mobile devices. This evolution from desktop to mobile has changed how people search online. The searcher typically has a different mindset when searching from their phone rather than a computer.

When people search on the phone, they usually want to take immediate action toward their goal, whether gathering information or getting their problem solved then and there. Of course, we know cosmetic treatments aren't available without advance notice, but that's ok. When it comes to med spa services, the searcher must feel like immediate action has been taken. Otherwise, when the searcher doesn't feel like action has been taken, they will simply go to the next provider shown on the search results page.

You can set up ad campaigns to build click-to-call into your mobile campaigns. It would be a mobile PPC campaign with the click-to-call function enabled. If someone hits the "Call" button, they immediately connect to that business. This is a quick and convenient alternative to having people go to a landing page for the phone number. And fast and convenient is just what mobile searchers want.

Plus, as you probably already know, there is not a lot of screen space on the phone. The sponsored listings become prominent, dominating the search results page on mobile. The top two positions often get a majority of the clicks on mobile. Again, it's all about convenience, and the click-to-call function supports that.

It's extremely powerful to connect with people searching from mobile devices. Set up a mobile-specific campaign and choose "Mobile Devices Only." You can pick your geolocation, which would be your radius. Then it's just a tap of a button to turn on the click-to-call function. By bidding correctly and enabling click-to-call, you can get your pay-per-click campaign in the top positions.

I'll go deeper into mobile optimization in an upcoming chapter.

Measuring the ROI of PPC Advertising

When running PPC campaigns, you want to monitor specific metrics so that you can adjust your PPC strategy if anything isn't performing well. In addition to the key metrics you should know, you'll want to measure the ROI and ROAS of your pay-per-click campaigns. Both formulas for calculating your ROI and ROAS require knowing the revenue generated from your PPC campaigns.

Return on Investment (ROI)

This formula will give you the ROI for your PPC campaign as a percentage. For example, if your total revenue from your PPC campaign is $10,000 and your total cost is $5,000, your ROI would be 100%.

ROI = (Total Revenue - Total Cost) / Total Cost

Return on Ad Spend (ROAS)

This formula will give you the ROAS for your PPC campaign as a percentage. For example, if your total revenue from your PPC campaign is $10,000 and your total cost is $5,000, then your ROAS would be 200%.

ROAS = (Total Revenue / Total Cost) * 100

In addition to these two formulas, there are a few other metrics that you can use to measure your ROI on PPC marketing. These metrics include:

Click-through rate (CTR): The percentage of people who see and click on your ad.

Conversion rate: The percentage of people who click on your ad and take a desired action, such as scheduling a consultation or signing up for your email list.

Cost per acquisition (CPA): The average amount of money you spend to acquire a new customer or lead.

Lifetime value (LTV): The total amount of money a customer or lead is worth to your business over their lifetime.

By tracking these metrics, you can better understand how your PPC campaigns perform and whether they generate a positive ROI.

Recap & Review

There was a lot to share in this chapter! Pay-per-click marketing is an excellent component of almost any marketing plan, but mistakes can be costly for a business. Use the information in this chapter to shield your practice from those costly mistakes and run successful campaigns that pay for themselves many times over.

To recap, you want to:

- Set up your ad groups correctly
- Select good keywords and group them together
- Write text ads that speak directly to the group of keywords

- Make your landing page specific to the ad text and the group of keywords
- Include a strong call to action that prompts action

Again, as the relevancy of your ad campaigns and keywords improve, your cost per click will decline, and your conversions will improve. You can spend less and still get better positioning and more traffic to your landing page. This is how you maximize the profitability of your pay-per-click marketing campaigns and succeed in PPC, where others fail.

CHAPTER 12

GET MAXIMUM RESULTS WITH SOCIAL MEDIA MARKETING

Level 2: Reach

- Search Engine Optimization (SEO)
- Optimized Content
- Google Maps Optimization
- Paid Ads
- **Social Media**

Social media has been around for years and has become a staple in marketing plans for almost every medical spa in business today. I've found that while most med spas can be found on social media platforms (Instagram, Facebook, TikTok, Twitter, YouTube, and LinkedIn), not all are actually leveraging social media to grow their practice.

In this chapter, we'll go over using social media marketing specifically to grow your medical spa. I hope that by now, you've learned a lot about how to position your company online, rank well in organic listings on Google Maps and in organic non-paid listings, and set up your paid ads for success. Now we'll layer in social media for massive results.

First, let's dive right into the "lowest-hanging fruit." The lifeblood of any service business is its existing customers, and medical spas are no different. Whether your patients are returning for multiple services over time or referring your practice to their friends and family, happy med spa clients typically love to share their "secret weapon" with others. When harnessed correctly, social media allows you to take repeat and referral business to a new level.

Let me explain why it's an excellent place for you to connect with your med spa clients and get more repeat and referral business.

Here are a few social media statistics from a quick Google search:

- 72.8% of internet users use social media for brand research
- The average time spent on social media is 2 hours and 24 minutes a day
- 70% of consumers look to Instagram for their next purchase

When your current and past patients (your sphere of influence) connect with you on social media, your business is exposed to their followers. It's almost as if your client sent an email or text to all their friends saying, "I recently received a service from this medical spa in our area. The next time you need a treatment they offer, why don't you consider them?" It's extremely powerful to gain exposure to their sphere of influence.

Another significant advantage is that connecting on social media platforms allows you to remain top-of-mind with them. Again, the average person spends almost two and a half hours on social media daily. If you're posting frequently, people will see your posts when they check in to scroll.

Top-of-Mind Awareness

There is a higher probability that folks who have liked your med spa profile will use your services again and refer you to their friends. They know your med spa and remember they had a good experience with you. You've remained top-of-mind.

If you look at major companies like Coca-Cola, Pepsi, and Lay's, they spend billions of dollars annually on advertising and promotions. They do that because they're developing their brand to maintain what we call "TOMA," or top-of-mind awareness. Leveraging social media inside your existing sphere of influence is a great way to tap into that top-of-mind awareness.

Relevant Social Media Platforms

With all of the social media platforms today, it can be hard to know where to start. Your med spa doesn't have to be on all these platforms to thrive. Knowing which ones will give you more bang for your buck is essential.

Instagram: Instagram is the most popular platform for med spas. It's an excellent platform for sharing your visual content, such as before-and-after photos of your treatments, images of your spa, and lifestyle photos that highlight the benefits of your services. Instagram is also a good way to connect with younger audiences.

Facebook: Facebook is still the most popular social media platform globally. You can use Facebook to share news about your spa, promote your services, and connect with potential clients. As a side note, Facebook is also a data point for Google. With your practice's location, phone number, and website published on your business page, Google sees that as supporting evidence that your business is legitimate.

YouTube: YouTube is a fantastic platform for sharing educational content about your treatments. You can create videos about the benefits of your treatments, how-to videos, and testimonials from your clients. YouTube is also beneficial to help you build your med spa's brand and authority.

TikTok: TikTok is a newer social media platform growing in popularity, especially among younger audiences. TikTok is an excellent platform for sharing short, engaging videos showcasing your treatments and spa.

Pinterest: Pinterest is a visual platform popular for inspiration and planning. You can use Pinterest to share images of your treatments, skincare tips, and lifestyle content. Pinterest can be a great way to reach potential clients in the early stages of planning their beauty treatments.

While these are the most relevant social media platforms for med spas, the best platform for your practice will depend on your target audience and marketing goals. However, all the platforms listed can effectively reach potential med spa clients and build your brand.

Building an Engaging Social Media Strategy

You'll first want to decide on a few elements to create your social media strategy. You've already identified your target audience, so skip outlining the types of content you want to share and your posting frequency. Then, research to discover the most effective hashtags for you and decide which metrics you will use to measure the success of your social media strategy. Lastly, have a plan in place to engage with your followers.

Types of Content

The types of content shared in your med spa's social media accounts will impact the effectiveness of your social media efforts.

- Before-and-after photos of clients who have had specific treatments
- Testimonials from happy clients
- Tips on how to best care for skin at home
- Lifestyle photos that highlight the benefits of your treatments

Sometimes knowing what *not* to post is more important than knowing what to post. The natural tendency is to go to these social media profiles and just post promotional material.

Using the 80-20 rule for social media messaging is a good idea: 80% of your content should be educational and entertaining. Only 20% should be promotional. If you post promotional content every time you log in, your followers will disappear before you know it, and your engagement will tank.

I don't recommend posting about your political or religious beliefs. Your beliefs are important, but it can create a hostile atmosphere if someone disagrees. You've got a personal profile for a reason. If you want to put your religious or political beliefs there, knock yourself out.

We used to keep all personal posts off business pages, but today, we know that bringing personal elements into your business profile helps people know, like, and trust you. Of course, don't plaster your business account with photos of your kids, family, or vacation photos. Still, in a limited number, these photos help show you as a complete human and not just a faceless business account.

Hashtags

Using relevant hashtags is extremely important when posting on specific social media platforms. It's how you can get your content to reach a wider audience. Because people can follow hashtags, your content shows up in the feeds of those following the hashtag, even when they're not explicitly following you.

The number of hashtags to use in a post is up for debate. Some will tell you to use as many as the platform will allow, while others say 3-5 hashtags per post is preferred. I recommend using as many as you feel comfortable with as long as you only use hashtags pertinent to the post.

According to Later, a social media posting tool, 20 hashtags is the magic number for the best reach, and 30 hashtags are ideal for the best engagement rate. Don't be afraid to experiment and see what works for you.

I recommend using a combination of hashtags related to "med spa," the treatment you're mentioning in your post, your location, lifestyle topics, and your brand. I have a spreadsheet listing several options for each category, including hashtags for each treatment. Then, when it's time to add hashtags to a post, it's easy to pull from my list of pre-vetted hashtags.

The table below shows a list of example hashtags in each category. If you'd like to download a copy of this spreadsheet to populate it with your hashtags, go to https://medspamarketingbook.com/free-resources.

Medspa	Treatment	Location	Lifestyle	Brand
#medspa	#LaserHairRemoval	#Seattle	#selflove	#yourmedspa
#medicalspa	#SmoothSkin	#SeattleWA	#confidence	#yourslogan
#skincare	#HairFree	#SeattleWashington	#selfcare	#womeninbusiness
#aesthetics	#PermanentHairRemoval	#SeattleGram	#glowup	#medspaowner
#skintreatment	#NoMoreShaving	#SeattleMedSpa	#pamperyourself	#medspalife
#antiaging	#LaserTreatment	#SeattleSkincare	#beauty	#aestheticnurseinjector
#healthyskin	#HairRemoval	#SeattleAesthetics	#BeautyRoutine	#injectorlife
#glowingskin	#HairFreeSkin	#SeattleBeautyTreatments	#SkincareGoals	#aestheticianlife
#noninvasive	#laserhairremovaltreatment	#SeattleGlow	#GlowingSkin	#aestheticmedicine
#beforeandafter	#HairRemovalJourney	#SeattleBeauty	#BeautyInspiration	#nursepractitionerlife

Posting Frequency

You should post new content regularly to keep your followers engaged. The frequency of your posts will depend on your platform, target audience, and growth goals. Some med spas are happy to post three times a week, while others work on aggressive growth and post thrice daily.

I believe consistency is a significant factor here. Regardless of how many posts you've published, your posts won't show up for your followers if you're not doing it consistently. If you have five posts to publish, you're far better off scheduling one per day for the next five days than scheduling all five to post today.

Find the frequency that works best for your practice and stick with it.

Believe it or not, sometimes posting content is the easiest part of this job. In addition to posting frequent content, you must engage. Social media isn't a one-way dialogue. The last thing you want to do is push out a bunch of posts without engagement. The objective here is to engage with your audience.

When & How to Engage

Engaging in social media is somewhat of a lost art. Most people that use social media just post one-way messages, which is not the idea. It's a social platform, so there should be conversation and dialogue.

An engaging social media strategy requires *engagement.* Using social media for your business is a social act, so you must reply to your follower's actions, thank people for following you, and give lots of attention to testimonials. It's important that you're not posting on social media just to post.

I've seen countless businesses that follow a good plan to post content but overlook engagement entirely. This is not the type of activity that you can do on a schedule and check a box that it's complete. Of course, you can add posts to your profiles on schedule, but social media aims to start conversations, which requires continuous monitoring and interaction.

When done right, social media is helpful to attract new clients, but it's also an excellent channel to connect with your established clients. It's a simple process—consistently publish educational and entertaining posts and engage with your followers. That's it in a nutshell. If you do this regularly and correctly, you will grow a nice following of real clients in your local area. Your medical spa will remain top-of-mind and help you grow your practice with repeat and referral business.

Advertising on Social Media

Paid ads on social media channels, such as Meta, YouTube, and TikTok, can be a fantastic addition to your med spa's marketing strategy. They are very different from Google Ads, though.

While Google Ads attract leads actively searching for your services, social media ads are interruption-based, as they target people not actively seeking your services. This fundamental difference in intent between the two platforms can significantly impact the effectiveness and approach of your marketing strategy.

With Google Ads, users are already in a proactive mindset, actively looking for solutions to their needs or problems. By strategically targeting relevant keywords, you can position your ads in front of users who have expressed explicit intent. When someone clicks on your Google ad, there's a higher likelihood that they are genuinely interested in your med spa services and are more likely to convert into a lead or customer.

On the other hand, social media ads aim to capture users' attention while they are engaged in socializing, entertainment, or browsing content. People typically visit social media platforms to connect with friends, consume content, or get updated on various topics of interest. They're not actively seeking services like those offered by a med spa. With this difference in intent and mindset, I believe social media ads are best for retargeting, promoting events, and brand awareness.

The key challenge with interruption-based advertising is to make an immediate impact and capture the audience's attention to stop the scroll. It requires creating ads that stand out amidst the sea of social media content and quickly convey the value and benefits of your med spa services.

To effectively leverage social media ads, creating compelling visual ad content that resonates with your target audience's interests and pain points is important. You can focus on sharing the unique aspects of your med spa, such as the ambiance, expertise of the staff, or testimonials from satisfied customers, showcase before-and-after results, and highlight the benefits of specific treatments.

Because social media platforms offer advanced targeting options, you can reach specific demographics, interests, and behaviors that align with your target audience. Targeting opportunities makes social media platforms valuable to your advertising efforts. The winning trifecta is smart targeting, compelling ad content, and ongoing optimization efforts. Experiment with different ad formats like image, video, or carousel ads to determine which types resonate best with your target audience.

While the intent behind Google Ads and social media ads differs, incorporating both into your marketing strategy can provide a comprehensive approach to reaching a wider range of potential clients. Google Ads can capture those actively searching for your services, while social media ads can help create brand awareness, generate interest, and nurture leads over time.

Measuring Social Media Success

Several metrics can be used to measure how well your social media efforts are working for your med spa. However, the metrics you want to use for your situation depend on your goals. There is minimal benefit, if any, to giving attention to metrics that don't align with your particular goals. So, always keep your goals for each ad campaign in mind as you evaluate the data.

Impressions: This metric indicates the number of times your ad was displayed to users on social media platforms. A higher number of impressions suggests increased visibility and reach.

Click-through Rate (CTR): CTR represents the percentage of people who clicked on your ad or post after seeing it. A higher CTR indicates your content is compelling and engaging, driving users to act.

Engagement Metrics: These include likes, comments, shares, and video views. These metrics reflect the level of audience engagement and indicate how well your content resonates with your target audience. Higher engagement suggests that your content is appealing and captivating.

Conversions: Conversions are actions that users take after clicking on your ad or post, such as booking an appointment, submitting a form, or making a purchase. Tracking conversions allows you to measure the direct impact of your social media ads on driving desired outcomes.

Cost Per Result: This metric calculates the average cost for each desired outcome, such as a conversion or a lead generated. It helps assess the efficiency and cost-effectiveness of your social media efforts.

Return on Ad Spend (ROAS): ROAS measures the revenue generated in relation to the amount spent on social media ads. It indicates the profitability of your ad campaigns and helps evaluate the return on your advertising investment.

Audience Insights: Social media platforms provide valuable data about your ad's audience, such as demographics, interests, and behaviors. Analyzing these insights can help refine your targeting strategy and tailor future campaigns to reach the most relevant audience.

Again, defining your goals and aligning your KPIs is essential. Whether it's increasing brand awareness, driving website traffic, or generating leads, selecting the most relevant metrics will provide insights into the specific objectives you want to achieve.

To measure these metrics, you can utilize the analytics and reporting tools provided by social media platforms themselves. These tools offer detailed data and reporting features to help track and assess the performance of your social media content and your ad campaigns.

As you monitor and analyze these metrics, you'll be able to evaluate the success of your social media efforts, identify areas for improvement, and optimize your campaigns for better results.

CHAPTER 13

USING VIDEO TO ENHANCE YOUR MEDSPA'S VISIBILITY & DRIVE CONVERSIONS

V ideo is the most powerful digital marketing tool available to us today. We all know video is highly effective in social media efforts, but video can also be leveraged for all your other marketing channels. Video enhances your SEO work, website, email campaigns, and more. The bottom line is that video helps expand your reach through whatever marketing channel you use.

Video marketing goes beyond stories and reels. Simply hosting your videos on YouTube helps your visibility and reach too. Did you know that YouTube is the second-largest search engine today? Yes, YouTube is technically a search engine, getting more searches than Bing!

So many medical spas are focused on search engine optimization but neglect the opportunities that video and YouTube provide. Implementing a video marketing strategy for your business can get you additional placement in the search results for your targeted keywords, enhance the effectiveness of your SEO efforts, and even improve visitor conversion.

Why Use Video Marketing?

There are several reasons to use video marketing for your med spa. First, it will increase your exposure for the most important keywords by giving your brand more "real estate" in the search engine results. Video marketing will enhance your SEO effort by driving visitors to your website and creating relevant links to your website, which will improve conversion.

Once somebody gets to your website, videos throughout the pages help visitors resonate more deeply than on a website without video. Your videos can help you connect with potential clients as you answer the very questions they're looking for answers to. This helps convert those visitors from browsing pages to picking up the phone and calling your office for a treatment appointment.

We're currently experiencing a time of massive opportunity. Video is consumed at an astounding rate, and there are no signs of it slowing down anytime soon. While a good percentage of medical spas have adopted video marketing strategies, there are still a ton of practices that haven't. This is the time to adapt or get left behind.

I mentioned that videos can give your brand more "real estate" in search engine results. The photo below is an example of how that works. Not only are your videos linked, just like any page on your website, but the search result also shows an image of your video next to the text. That's a big "click here" message in today's visual world. Plus, with video, you now have more chances to show multiple search results. That makes it much easier for you to dominate the search results for your keywords.

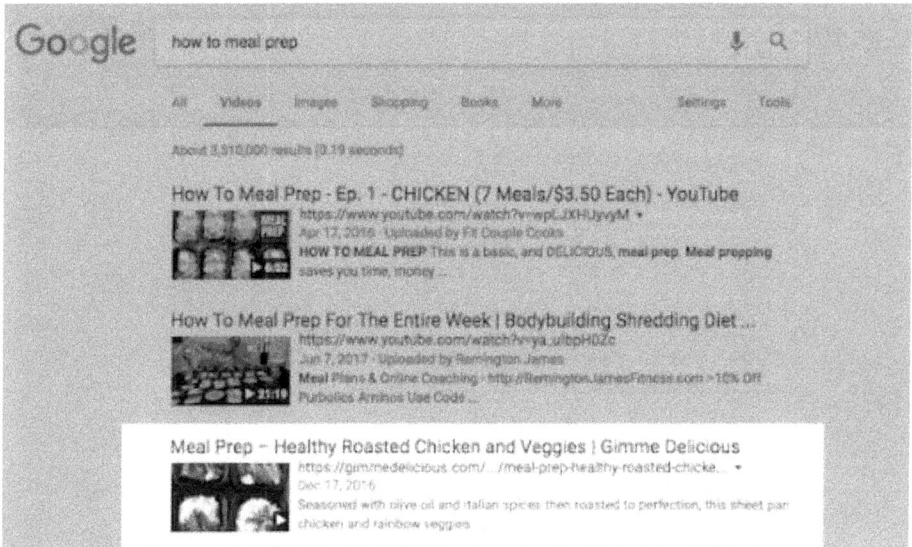

This website, gimmedelicious.com, really likes to focus on meal preparation. This particular blog explains the basics of meal prep. If we type in a search on Google for "How to meal prep," you'll see that their video shows up on page one with a few other listings. If you click that link, it takes you straight to a video.

In this case, the blog post is optimized for meal prep. As a result, both the website and accompanying videos appear in organic search results. This can be observed through various keywords that are used. By ensuring proper optimization, your website will be visible, and your video will also have the opportunity to appear in relevant searches.

If you optimize your videos correctly (I'll show you exactly how in this chapter), you can start to have your videos show up in the organic search results on Google, which is extremely powerful. And, of course, having multiple results show up in organic searches gives you a fantastic advantage.

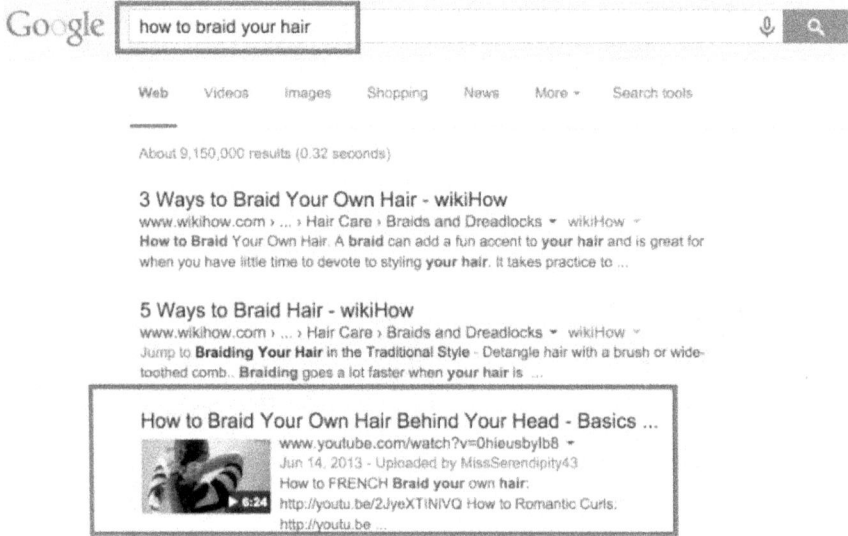

Another example is this YouTube video that describes hair braiding. If you type in "How to braid your hair," you will find that the Wikihow website ranks first and second, followed directly by a video.

Whether your video ranks number one, two, or three, the video will get a much higher clickthrough rate most of the time. This is likely because of the image displaying what the video is. A lot of attention goes to video results.

Read on to learn how to incorporate these videos for your med spa treatments and optimize them to show up like this in your market.

Video Supports SEO Efforts

The other thing we can accomplish with video is enhancing our SEO efforts. As covered in the SEO chapter, links are critical for ranking. Good video content lets you generate inbound links to your website from high-level video sites like YouTube and Vimeo.

As you add videos to YouTube, don't make the mistake of linking all of your videos to your homepage. You want to link your videos to your core services or treatment pages. Videos that link to those internal pages will help your SEO efforts.

Another advantage related to SEO is that video content on your website reduces your bounce rate and increases visitors' time. These are both important SEO factors.

"Bounce rate" refers to how often someone gets to your web page and clicks back out immediately without taking any other action on the page. Google interprets this action as the page not being relevant to the search. If the majority of people that get to your site leave right away, your bounce rate will be high, and Google will start to show your website less prominently in the results. That's part of Google's algorithm.

The other factor is the amount of time spent on the site. If someone gets to your web page, stays there for ten seconds, and clicks out, the visit might not get treated like a bounce, but Google is still considering the time spent on the site.

If you have a video on the page and a visitor takes the time to watch it, that improves the metrics for visitors' time on your site. Even if they only watch a few seconds of the video, you have captured their attention long enough that Google will see your site is relevant.

Don't get confused by the notion that having videos on your website automatically improves your SEO—that's not necessarily the case. But having people stay on your web page longer and not bounce off does impact SEO.

I've mentioned that video can give you more placement in search engine results. It will improve your website's search engine optimization because you get links from the video sites, increasing visitors' time while reducing the bounce rate. But the most powerful benefit of video is that it will improve conversion.

You can have the best SEO strategy in the world and drive hundreds of people looking for the treatments your medical spa provides to your homepage or internal treatment pages. But, if your website isn't converting and visitors aren't picking up the phone or submitting a form to schedule a treatment or a consultation, you're missing a major opportunity.

Improving Conversion with Video

Improving conversion is one of the main things having intelligent video on your site will do for you. The fact is that video clips resonate with people. People like video because it allows them to get to know, like, and trust you before they call your practice, especially if you follow the strategy I will share with you rather than creating a super corporate video.

If you make authentic videos of you and your team talking directly to the camera, connecting with them emotionally, answering questions, and giving a strong call to action, your conversion rate will improve.

Video also gives you the ability to connect with different modalities. Everybody thinks differently. Some people are readers and will read all the content on a page. Some people are listeners, so if they can listen to something rather than read, they'll choose to listen. Other people like something visual. Motion grabs their eye. You can connect with every type of person by having video on your website, combined with text (I'm not saying to abandon text).

What Videos to Make

So, you now understand that video is powerful. Video will improve your SEO, help your website get better placement in search engines, and could help with conversion. With this in mind, you may wonder what your next steps should be.

You'll want to create simple videos about your practice, the treatments you offer, and the most frequently asked questions. You can create videos about almost any topic you want, but the videos that pertain to your services will be the most relevant.

The first video that I recommend you make is an introduction video for your website. An example of a simple script for the video is below:

Thank you for visiting the XYZ Medical Spa website. We specialize in providing XYZ treatments to the XYZ area. Our patients choose us because...

- *Unique selling point 1*
- *Unique selling point 2*
- *Unique selling point 3*

We'd love the opportunity to serve you. Call us at the number below, and we can schedule you for a consultation or treatment right away.

The other videos you want to create should be about your primary treatments or services. This ties in well with the SEO strategy discussed previously. You want to ensure you have a page on your website for each treatment or service you provide. Make a list of the services you want to attract more business and shoot a brief video about each.

Once you've completed the treatment videos, phase two is recording videos that share your answers to frequently asked questions. These FAQ videos are powerful content. List the questions people tend to ask and create a video about each. A few examples include:

How long do CoolSculpting® results last?

What exactly does BOTOX® do?

What is Juvederm best for?

How often should you do microneedling?

This is common information to you, but the average client doesn't know. Creating a simple video providing answers to your patients' frequently asked questions makes for great video content for your YouTube channel to be syndicated on your social media profiles and uploaded to your blog on your website.

I find the best way to prepare for recording videos is to have notes with bullet points you want to cover. Writing out a full script tends to make videos feel less natural or authentic to viewers. You want to speak as naturally to the camera as possible, just like you would to a client in person.

You should always include a call to action telling viewers what to do. If you feel comfortable with it, referencing a discount can go a long way too, but it's not a requirement for a good video.

Don't overthink this! Think about the core services that you offer. Shoot a quick 30- to 90-second video about each, and you're ready to roll.

YouTube Best Practices

Now that you have completed shooting your videos, you can share them with the world. If you don't already have a YouTube channel, your next step is to set one up.

When you set up your YouTube channel, go into the settings and complete everything you can. You want to use every advantage you can to help get your videos to show up in the search results on both YouTube and Google.

Ensure you give your channel a "city + service - name of your medical spa" title instead of just your business name. YouTube gives you the ability to add channel keywords. You have up to 500 characters available to you, so be sure to add your most important keywords such as "your city medspa," "your city medical spa," "your city cosmetic treatments," and, of course, your company name.

Then go into the Customization area in your YouTube account. Add your company logo as your YouTube profile photo, and if you have a picture that will work for your banner image, add that too. Add a description of your business under the "Basic Info" section. Make sure to include your business name, address, and phone number the same as it is in your Google Maps listing and everywhere else online. As we covered in the

Google Maps Optimization chapter, citation development is critical. YouTube is a fantastic citation source.

Again, fill out as much information as you can. Make a note of any fields that you want to return to later. For example, YouTube allows you to spotlight a channel trailer to show to users who haven't subscribed to your channel and a featured video for returning subscribers. Those are great features that I recommend taking advantage of, but you can add them later.

Before you upload your videos to YouTube, name each one correctly and intelligently, including terms people will use to search for the topic. If somebody is looking for a BOTOX® provider, they type in something like "your city botox." You want to name the video using those words. For example, "Seattle botox."

Uploading Videos to YouTube

Now, you have the inventory of videos I recommended: an intro video and clips for each of your services. You have your YouTubnel set up, and you've added your business details. It's time to upload your videos, and there are some important steps to follow to ensure your videos have the most impact on your business.

Video Title: "City + service - Company," but mix this up a bit so your titles aren't always the same. For the service, use your primary keyword(s). Using "microneedling" as an example for the imaginary "Radiant Rejuvenation Medspa" in Seattle, the video title would be "Seattle Microneedling - Radiant Rejuvenation Medspa." You must have the correct titles on your videos to help Google locate and include them in search results.

Video Description: At the beginning of the description, add a URL to the correct page. With the "microneedling" example above, the video would link to your microneedling page. Use the entire URL, including "https://." Then briefly outline what the video says and include the exact words you used in your title. Continuing with the same example, you would have "Seattle microneedling" in the description. **Always add**

your NAP (name, address, phone number) at the bottom of the description.

Tags: Add your most important keywords for the particular treatment as tags. Again, YouTube allows you to add up to 500 characters here, so take advantage of each character. Remember to include your location.

Thumbnail: Select a thumbnail photo for your video. Think of it like a book cover. You can upload a picture if you have a relevant image, but you can also select an image from the video once it's fully uploaded.

Location: In the advanced settings, there is a field to add your med spa's location. Add your unique address. You'll see a dropdown with your options as you type it out. Your website address should be at the top, including "https://."

YouTube's Embed Code

Now that you've uploaded your video and properly optimized it, your title is correct, and your description is posted, it's time to leverage them for more impact. You need videos posted on your website and social media profiles to get the full benefit of this conversion component.

You'll want to use YouTube's embed code to add the videos to your website. Go to the video you want to post on your website and choose the share and embed option. You'll need to copy the small piece of code for your specific video. I've highlighted the embed code in the example below. If you are updating your website independently, copy and paste the code into your website's HTML. If you have a web manager, send the code off to them with details on where you want it posted.

Embed Video   ✕

```
<iframe width="560" height="315"
src="https://www.youtube.com/embed/yA
8DXvl99n8" title="YouTube video
player" frameborder="0"
allow="accelerometer; autoplay;
clipboard-write; encrypted-media;
gyroscope; picture-in-picture; web-
share" allowfullscreen></iframe>
```

☐ Start at

EMBED OPTIONS

☑ Show player controls

☐ Enable privacy enhanced mode ⓘ

Copy

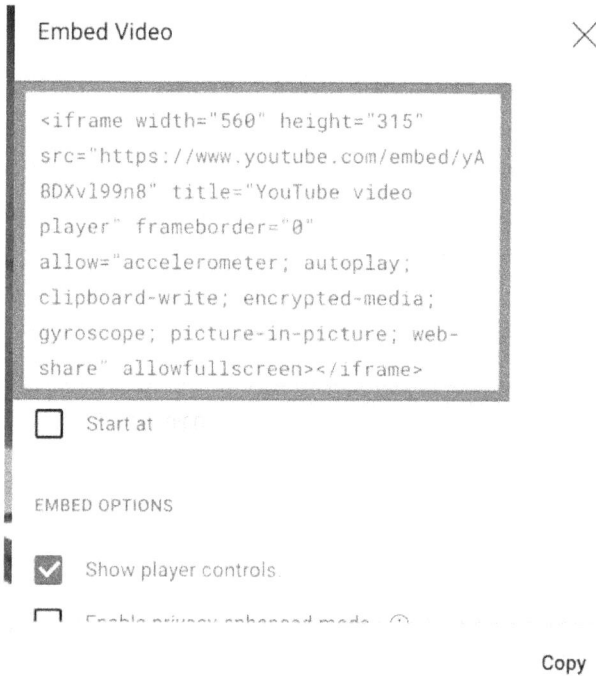

Remember, the introduction video should be embedded on your website's homepage, and the service-specific videos should be on the appropriate internal services pages.

Don't Overthink It

A lot of people struggle with video. I know I did for a long time. But video is so powerful you can let the struggle stop you, or you can decide to reap the benefits from it. As I mentioned before, people resonate with people. So keep it simple, be authentic, personable, and to the point. You're not trying to create 20-minute videos at first. An appropriate length would be 30 seconds to three minutes, just long enough to get your message across.

Don't overthink it! You don't need to go all out and hire a high-end production crew or buy an HD camera to make this happen. In reality, you can create video clips using technology you already have. If you've got a smartphone or a webcam, you can create video content that will work for your website.

You don't need high-end editing software, either. YouTube allows you to upload regular video and edit it within the system. By edit, I mean cropping and tailoring the video to begin and end where you wish. You can put your phone number down in the bottom area of the video as well as a link to your website. Or you can use simple editing software like iMovie (free with Mac computers) or Movie Maker (free with PCs).

Using the technology that you already have, stand in front of a company sign with your logo or in your office and simply talk to the camera. Talk with the people that are visiting your website because that's going to stick with them.

CHAPTER 14

ENGAGE CLIENTS & LEADS WITH POWERFUL EMAIL & SMS COMMNICATIONS

Level 3: Repeat

- **Email Newsletters**
- **Reactivation Campaigns**
- **Cross-Selling Services**

Level 3 is all about email & SMS marketing. While there are three different marketing strategies at this level, there is a lot of overlap in the information you need to know to be successful, so I include them all together in this chapter. Before I go into the three strategies, I want to give you a general understanding of email and SMS marketing.

Ever since there's been email, there's been email marketing. Email marketing is one of the oldest forms of digital marketing for businesses. Even though people sometimes negatively associate it with spam, email marketing remains one of the most impactful marketing methods.

I'm a big believer in email marketing. It's a powerful way to get instant traffic to your website and generate inquiries. However, it's crucial to acknowledge that there are right and wrong approaches when employing this strategy.

Did you know the easiest customer to sell to is the customer you already have?

Every self-proclaimed marketing expert will tell you that's nothing new. But many businesses don't keep in touch with their existing client base. Companies will spend thousands of dollars trying to get new customers but ignore marketing to the clients who already buy from them.

Why is that? I have a lot of ideas about this. I suspect business owners think that once customers buy from them, they will just return on their own. Or maybe they simply don't want to bother their clients.

While this is prevalent across all industries, it's especially unfortunate in aesthetics. Few types of services are as well-suited to email marketing as those offered by med spas and other aesthetic providers.

The truth is clients want to hear from you, and they want to be engaged by your practice. If you don't, your competition will.

Building & Managing a Client Database

I am regularly asked about how to get email addresses. It's not as easy as sending a snail-mail letter through the USPS to anyone you want to. The reality is that simply having a client's email address does not permit you to send them anything you want. It's crucial to obtain their consent before sending any marketing emails.

It can be confusing because you already have their email address, and they have used your services before, so isn't it ok to add them to your marketing email list? Technically, no. While you have permission to send a person transactional emails, you must obtain their permission to send emails with commercial intent.

First, you want your clients' permission to add them to your email list. There are a variety of ways to do this, including having a checkbox on any website forms, displaying a form on your website that's specific to subscribing to your marketing emails, and even asking people if they'd like to subscribe when they are making an appointment or checking out after a treatment.

Explain that your emails are where you roll out the red carpet for your VIPs. Your VIPs receive exclusive discounts and monthly specials; they're the first to know about upcoming events. You might even offer a special promotion if they subscribe. Getting that email address is extremely valuable, so even if it costs you, go for it.

Remember, you want to have your medical spa's name in front of your clients every month. Even if they're not taking advantage of the specials you're sharing, your med spa will be top-of-mind when they need treatment or if one of their friends is looking for cosmetic treatments that your practice provides.

Overall, staying in touch with established patients can help you build stronger relationships with your patient base, increase revenue, and grow your med spa over time. Start building your email list today!

Personalization & Segment Strategies

The impact personalization and segmenting your client list can have on the success of your email marketing can't be emphasized enough. When medical spas come to me with disappointing email marketing results, it's almost always because these important strategies are overlooked.

Studies indicate that 39% of consumers are more likely to spend more on products and services when emails are personalized. Emails are more likely to be opened, read, and acted upon when personalised and tailored to the recipient's interests. This can lead to higher conversion rates, increased customer loyalty, and greater lifetime value for your clients.

Personalization

In email and SMS marketing, personalization refers to tailoring your messages to individual recipients' unique preferences, needs, and characteristics. It goes beyond simply addressing subscribers by name (although that's an essential component).

Personalization involves leveraging data, insights, and client segmentation to deliver highly relevant content, offers, and experiences to each subscriber. This personalized approach has several significant benefits, with relevance and engagement at the top of the list.

By personalizing your email campaigns, you can deliver content related to your subscribers' favorite treatments, skincare concerns, or wellness goals. This relevance goes beyond improving click-through rates and conversions of your campaigns. It instills trust, positioning your medical spa as the go-to source for personalized advice and solutions.

Personalization is achieved by segmenting your client list.

Segmentation

Segmenting your email list allows you to deliver relevant content and promotions that align with each subscriber's preferences. Studies indicate that 39% of consumers are more likely to spend more on products and services when emails are personalized.

Quality data is king to get the best results from your email marketing campaigns. When you want to know which levers to pull to create results, the data tells you everything you need to know. But data doesn't show up on its own. You need to set things up so that the data provides the right details. That's where segmenting comes in.

To have the ability to personalize and segment your contact list, I recommend all med spas have the following minimum data points for each contact:

- First name
- Gender
- Birthday
- Total number of visits
- Date of last visit
- Treatments purchased
- Email subscriber: Y/N

Once you have this information, personalization and segmentation can revolutionize your email marketing efforts!

If you're just starting with segmentation, begin with the information you already have in your contact records. You can always add more data points later. Segmenting is an ongoing process that is never complete. So take it one step at a time, and your med spa will reap the rewards over time.

Key Metrics in Email Marketing

In email marketing, several key metrics are commonly used to measure the effectiveness and success of email campaigns. These metrics provide insights into how subscribers engage with your emails and help you optimize your strategies for better results. Here are some of the key metrics in email marketing:

Open Rate: The open rate represents the percentage of recipients who opened your email. It indicates the effectiveness of your subject line and helps you understand how engaging your emails are.

Click-Through Rate (CTR): CTR is the percentage of recipients who clicked on a link within your email. It measures the effectiveness of your email content and call-to-action (CTA). A higher CTR indicates better engagement.

Conversion Rate: The conversion rate measures the percentage of subscribers who took a desired action, such as making a purchase, signing up for a webinar, or downloading a resource after clicking on a link in your email. It helps evaluate the effectiveness of your email in driving desired outcomes.

Bounce Rate: The bounce rate represents the percentage of emails not delivered to recipients' inboxes. There are two types of bounces: hard bounces (permanent delivery failures) and soft bounces (temporary delivery issues). A high bounce rate may indicate problems with your email list quality or delivery infrastructure.

Unsubscribe Rate: The unsubscribe rate shows the percentage of subscribers who opted out or unsubscribed from your email list after receiving your email. It's essential to monitor this metric as it can reflect the relevance and quality of your content.

Spam Complaint Rate: This metric indicates the number of recipients who marked your email as spam. High spam complaint rates can harm your sender reputation and deliverability. Monitoring and minimizing this rate is crucial for maintaining good email deliverability.

List Growth Rate: The list growth rate measures the rate at which your email list expands. It's important to track this metric to grow your subscriber base and maintain a healthy list continuously.

ROI (Return on Investment): ROI measures the financial return generated from your email marketing efforts. It considers factors such as revenue from conversions, cost of email creation, and distribution. A positive ROI indicates a successful campaign.

By keeping an eye on these metrics and carefully studying the data, you'll be able to uncover valuable insights about how your email marketing campaigns are performing. These insights will guide you in making informed decisions, helping you fine-tune your strategies for even better outcomes in the future.

Creating Engaging Email Newsletters

When deciding what to send to your email list, use the 80/20 rule—80% information and 20% sales. If you only send emails about the treatments you offer, you'll have lackluster results and likely a lot of unsubscribes. People want to know about the opportunities but never want to feel sold to.

When writing the informational 80% of your emails, provide genuinely valuable information. This may include industry trends, skincare tips, new treatments, or client success stories. Whether you imagine sharing the news with a specific client, yourself, or your friends, ask yourself if it would interest you. If not, keep brainstorming topics.

For the 20% of your newsletter focused on sales, share a promotional offer with a clear expiration date, which will get those appointments booked now. I like to reward email subscribers with the best promotions available, but that doesn't mean constantly discounting one-off treatments. Get creative with promotions that give patients a deal while increasing their overall spending.

How Often to Send Email Campaigns

The cadence of your email campaigns is very important for engagement. Send too many emails, and people will quickly unsubscribe. Send too few emails, and you're not keeping your medical spa or your client's skincare goals top of mind.

I recommend medical spas send emails once to twice monthly. If you're just starting your email marketing system and doing it on your own, start with once per month. Once you feel comfortable with that, add one more monthly email to your plan and space the two out so people receive an email every couple of weeks.

When it comes to email marketing, consistency is crucial. So commit to the number of emails that works for you but be careful not to over-estimate your ability to get them out regularly. If you're just starting with email campaigns, writing, formatting, and sending them will probably take longer than expected.

The Best Time to Send Emails

To ensure your email has the best opportunity for engagement, the timing of your email campaigns is equally important. The best time to send email campaigns is dependent on several factors. However, the email marketing community widely accepts these general tips on when to send emails. They are great when you're starting, but **be sure to read on and see why they won't always work.**

Day-Time vs. Night-Time: While this one may be obvious, sending email campaigns during the daytime is usually better—you know, when people are awake and not asleep.

Mad Mondays: The consensus is that you should avoid sending email blasts on Mondays. After the weekend, people are flooded with emails they've collected over the past few days. What's the first thing they do? Delete those emails, of course!

Weekends: Historically, weekends are the days when folks are out running errands and going on adventures. Weekends tend to have low open rates, so most marketers avoid them like the plague.

Fan Favorites (Tuesday, Wednesday, and Thursday): These days have traditionally been favorite days to send email campaigns, as email marketers seek to avoid the Monday angst and Friday's itchy feet.

Reactivation Campaigns

Reactivation campaigns are a powerful marketing tool to increase sales and the average lifetime value of clients. Successful reactivation campaigns use email and SMS to re-engage clients who haven't received services in a specified time. Through reactivation campaigns, you remind clients of your beneficial treatments and entice them back with a well-crafted promotion.

One of the central components of these campaigns is the offer itself. While generalized offers can produce adequate responses, tailoring your promotions to align with your client's interests and needs dramatically increases the chance of re-engaging them.

Consider the example of a client who previously received BOTOX® injections but hasn't returned in 6 months. A reactivation campaign offering a tempting deal on another BOTOX® treatment is likely far more appealing than a general discount on any service. The SMS reactivation messages below are examples of general and personalized campaigns. Again, both work, but your results will be far better with the personalized campaign.

General Reactivation Campaign

It's been a while since your last visit to Renew Medspa. We miss you, and we have a special offer just for you! Enjoy a 10% discount on your next treatment if you book within 48 hours. Call us at [Phone Number] or reply YES to book your appointment.

We look forward to seeing you again!

Personalized Reactivation Campaign

Lisa, it's been a while since your last BOTOX® treatment at Renew Medspa. We miss you, and we have a special offer just for you! Enjoy a 20% discount on your next BOTOX® session if you book in the next 48 hours. Call us at [Phone Number] or reply YES to book your appointment.

We look forward to seeing you again!

It's also important to note that reactivation promotions can be a bit more aggressive than regular deals. Inactive clients have various reasons for not returning, but one common reason is that they've started receiving services from a competitor. A strong incentive to encourage them to prioritize a return visit is sometimes necessary to win them back from the competition.

As you can see in the examples, we included a time limit to create a sense of urgency. Time-limited offers, such as "book within 48 hours" or "limited-time discount," can motivate clients to take action quickly. You don't want to leave the promotion open-ended so that people have no incentive to book now. Always include a time limit!

You'll send a well-designed email from your email marketing platform to incorporate email into the reactivation campaign. The messaging is essentially the same, but you must use a strong subject line with the email. The subject line has one job—to compel the user to open the email. Here are a few examples of strong subject lines:

- We miss you! Come back and get __% off your next treatment.
- We've got a special offer just for you!
- It's been a while. We'd love to see you again!
- Book your appointment today and get __% off.

To launch successful reactivation campaigns for your med spa, you'll need a comprehensive client database that includes key contact information, such as email addresses and cell phone numbers, with consent to receive text messages. The ideal list will also include the history of treatments each client has received, which provides the necessary insights to personalize your offers.

If you don't have a client database like this, it's never too late to start. Over time, you'll collect the client data needed to use reactivation campaigns as a powerful tool that contributes to the growth of your medical spa.

Cross-Selling Services

Congratulations on reaching the final step of the 3R Medspa Marketing System! Cross-selling is a powerful strategy that can significantly boost your med spa's revenue while providing your clients with enhanced and personalized experiences. Cross-selling should be a part of your in-person sales strategies. Your practitioners and front desk staff are uniquely positioned to use consultative sales techniques, but that is a topic for another day or another book.

Your medical spa can use digital marketing as a powerful tool to promote cross-selling opportunities. With a segmented client database, you can communicate directly with clients to spotlight complementary treatments. Whether you utilize email or SMS campaigns, the key is to pique their interest in other treatments they may benefit from.

When using email campaigns, showcase the treatments and share success stories from happy clients who have experienced the benefits of the treatment you're cross-selling. For example, a client receiving regular BBL treatments will be an excellent candidate for MOXI.

Motivate your clients to explore complementary treatments by offering attractive incentives. Consider providing discounts or loyalty rewards for clients who book cross-sold treatments during a limited time.

To measure the success of your cross-selling efforts, keep track of key performance indicators (KPIs), such as the percentage of clients who opt for cross-sold treatments and the overall revenue generated through cross-selling. Analyze the data regularly to identify trends and optimize your cross-selling strategies based on the data.

Cross-selling should be integral to your med spa's digital marketing efforts. Remember, even though digital marketing is the vehicle to increase sales, the key to effective cross-selling is prioritizing your client's needs and delivering exceptional experiences that keep them returning for more.

CHAPTER 15

OPTIMIZE YOUR ONLINE PRESENCE FOR TODAY'S MOBILE USERS

On average, 65% of your website visitors are on a mobile device rather than a desktop, laptop, or tablet, so optimizing your marketing efforts for mobile is crucial. Technology and digital marketing are advancing at an astonishing rate and aren't expected to slow down anytime soon. This alone is causing many companies to be left behind.

Here are a few telling statistics about mobile that you should be aware of:

- Mobile devices account for 41.9% of all opened emails. (Litmus)
- 42.3% of people will delete an email not optimized for mobile. (SaleCycle)

- The number of searches for "near me" has increased by over 500% in recent years. (BusinessDIT)
- In 2023, Americans check their phones an average of 144 times daily. (Reviews.org)
- Almost 89% of surveyed users check their phones within 10 minutes of waking up. (Reviews.org)
- 57% of users won't recommend a business if their mobile website design is bad. (Forbes)

Everything we do, from your website and paid ads to emails, online forms, and everything else, must be optimized for mobile, or your results will suffer. I'll share my thoughts on a few specific channels below.

Mobile-Optimized Websites

The easiest way to see how your clients and potential clients are experiencing your website is to simply pull it up on your mobile phone. Go through the pages and forms to see what it's like for others.

Did your website load quickly? Was it easy to find your contact information and other details visitors look for when they're on the go? Was it optimized to fit your phone screen? If so, you've invested in your practice by ensuring your mobile clients and prospects are cared for. Well done!

If navigating your website is a nightmare, your phone is not the problem—it's your website. This means you have been losing potential business.

SMS Marketing

SMS marketing, also called text message marketing, is one of the most cost-effective and results-oriented forms of marketing today. Text message marketing allows you to draw in local clients with a great offer. Then you can send occasional messages or promotional offers to keep them returning for more treatments.

To ensure your SMS marketing efforts are as effective as possible, invite clients to take advantage of a specific offer and include a clear call to action (CTA) that's easy to execute on the go. You also want to use your client's name to personalize your message and keep it short and sweet—typically, no more than 160 characters.

Remember, SMS marketing gets your messages into a sacred space. Use that privilege wisely, and you'll reap the rewards.

Mobile Email Marketing

Email marketing designed for mobile viewers is an essential strategy in today's digital landscape. The key to effective mobile email marketing is creating emails that are easily readable, visually appealing, and interactive on smaller screens.

The design of mobile emails needs to prioritize simplicity to keep the layout clean and uncluttered. This includes using a single-column format with clear headings and concise text that helps users easily digest the information. The design must also be responsive to adapt the email layout to fit different screen sizes automatically.

Optimization is crucial for mobile email marketing. From compressing images and using HTML5 for videos to ensure fast loading times to designing buttons and links with sufficient spacing and sizing, every element must be optimized for the best user experience. Otherwise, users may have a frustrating experience with slow load times and accidental clicks on interactive elements that aren't spaced properly.

Evaluating Competitors' Mobile Strategies

Before you develop a mobile arsenal to drive more inbound calls, it's a good idea to figure out who your mobile competitors are. That way, you know who you are up against in mobile marketing and can plan your strategies accordingly. To do this effectively, you need to identify your closest competitors and learn what mobile techniques they use to generate their sales.

Start with their websites. It's easy to find out which competitors have a mobile-optimized website. Just search on your phone for any keywords, such as "medical spa," "med spa," or cosmetic treatment. Tap through the competitor websites in the search results. Look at their pages, try out the navigation, and click on forms. Interact with the website as anyone would expect to.

A word of caution: Spying on your competitors is not illegal, but there are limits you should follow to remain fair. Under no circumstances should you use unethical measures to jeopardize your competition in any way. Don't click on paid ads at the top of the search results. Advertisers pay for every click, so be fair.

Next, figure out which of your competitors are using SMS marketing. If your competitors do it, they probably tell the world to "text 123 to example." If you see promotions like this, they are definitely using text messaging to build a list of repeat clients.

There are several other forms of mobile marketing your competitors could be using to capture the attention of local clients, such as mobile SEO, QR codes, and mobile apps. If they use these methods, it may be in your best interest to start researching how your business can do it even better.

Evaluating Your Mobile Strategies

Researching your competition's strategies is necessary if your goal is to become the best-known med spa in your area. But it is equally important to analyze where your business stands to move forward. So many med spa owners put a lot of effort into competing with other med spas while neglecting to examine what their practice is doing closely.

Analyzing your mobile efforts' status will help you determine which weaknesses are holding your practice back and which strengths can help your med spa win the coveted top spot. It's essential to note what you are and aren't doing to generate more sales using mobile marketing.

The following questions will help you evaluate your medical spa's current mobile marketing status.

- Is your website mobile-friendly?
- Does your website load on your mobile phone within seconds, or does it take forever to render properly?
- Does your mobile website have all the relevant information consumers seek while on the go?
- Do the forms on your website work properly on mobile devices?
- Does your mobile website come up high in search engine results, or is it nowhere to be found when potential clients search for "treatment + city" on their mobile devices?
- If you're currently running Google Ads, are they optimized for mobile searches?
- Have you started to build an SMS marketing list?
- If so, what are you currently doing with your list of SMS subscribers?
- Do you have an opt-in/call to action on your printed and web marketing materials?
- Do you have an email marketing list?
- If so, what are you currently doing with your list of email subscribers?
- Are you ensuring any marketing campaigns sent are optimized for mobile?
- Are you using QR codes as an additional method of increasing awareness about your business?
- Do you have your QR codes on all your other marketing materials? Are you using them to direct traffic to your mobile website?
- Do you currently use a mobile app to keep your audience engaged?

As you can see, many things must be considered to ensure your practice is on the right track with mobile marketing.

Every medical spa in your local area is determined to get more clients, more booked appointments, and more profits. If you want your med spa to be a leader in your area, you simply can't ignore mobile marketing. Today's clients expect a mobile-friendly experience and won't stand for anything less.

CHAPTER 16

TRACK, MEASURE, & QUANTIFY TO ENSURE A STRONG ROI

Tracking and data play a vital role in digital marketing for med spas. By collecting and analyzing the right data, you can make informed decisions about your marketing strategies, improve your ROI, and continuously improve the online experience for your clients.

By tracking metrics related to website traffic, social media and email engagement, and conversions, you can better understand your audience's interests, demographics, and behavior. This information allows you to create personalized and impactful marketing campaigns that resonate with your clients and potential clients on a more personal level.

By monitoring what drives traffic to your website, generates leads, and leads to sales, you can make data-driven decisions to optimize your campaigns and maximize your return on investment (ROI). This is a tremendous advantage for med spas that utilize tracking because it empowers you to focus your efforts on the strategies and channels that yield the best results.

In addition to campaign performance, all medical spas should track client feedback. You can identify areas where improvements are needed by paying attention to client behavior and feedback, such as high bounce rates or frequent exits from the website without completing a purchase. This valuable data guides you in making your website more user-friendly, informative, and engaging.

It's important to remember that a website is never truly done. Data gives you the information you need to continuously improve the online experience for established and potential clients. Marketing is all about a test and tweak cycle on repeat to get the very best results possible.

Here are some specific examples of how you can use tracking and data in your med spa's digital marketing:

- Track website traffic to see where your visitors are coming from and what pages they view. This information can be used to identify your most popular content and target your marketing campaigns to the right people.

- Track social media engagement to see which posts get the most likes, shares, and comments. This information can be used to create more engaging content that will help you reach more people.

- Track email open and click-through rates to see how effective your email marketing campaigns are. This information can be used to improve your email content and subject lines.

- Track lead generation to see how many people are signing up for your email list or scheduling appointments. This information can be used to measure the effectiveness of your marketing campaigns and identify which channels drive the most leads.

- Track sales to see how much money you make from digital marketing efforts. This information can be used to calculate your ROI and ensure your marketing campaigns are profitable.

Analytics Tracking

Again, by tracking and analyzing the right data, you can gain incredibly valuable insights that will help to improve your digital marketing strategies and your business. This valuable information can be used to improve your digital marketing strategies and achieve your business goals.

Let's look at how you can track the data. You'll need to put some tools in place to track, measure, and quantify your data to ensure you're moving in a positive direction.

There are different tracking tools that you can put in place. I'm going to recommend three core tracking systems that will serve you well:

- Google Analytics
- Keyword Tracking
- Call Tracking

Google Analytics

Google Analytics is a completely free tool for analyzing your website data. Google Analytics will show you specifically:

- How many visitors get to your website on a daily, weekly, monthly, and annual basis
- What keywords they typed in to get there
- What pages on your website they visited
- How long they stayed

At first, the main thing you want to see from Google Analytics is where you started and are now. Maybe when you started, your website traffic was 5, 20, 100, or 500; whatever it was, that's a benchmark you can compare to future data on an ongoing basis. Eventually, you'll set a new benchmark, which will come later.

Ultimately, you want to see that your marketing efforts are moving things in a positive direction:

- Has the number of visitors to your website increased?
- Is the variety of keywords that they're finding you with growing?
- Is the website data moving in a positive direction?

You can also set up reports within Google Analytics. To get set up with Google Analytics, go to google.com/analytics. It's a relatively simple process. You verify that you own the website through various methods and then install a small piece of code into your website's HTML. After you have done that, you've got the tracking in place and are ready to go.

Keyword Tracking

The other tracking mechanism that I recommend is keyword tracking. At the beginning of this process, we discussed keyword research to determine what keywords people type in when they need your services. We created a list, and all those keywords were combined with the city your practice is located in.

Some tools will tell you how you rank on Google and Bing Desktop and mobile searches for those keywords. A few options include:

- BrightLocal
- SEMRush
- Advanced Web Ranking
- Whitespark

The keyword tracking tool I recommend is called BrightLocal. You can learn more about it at brightlocal.com. This service has a cost but is an excellent resource for tracking your search engine optimization progress.

You enter your keywords into BrightLocal's Keyword Tracker and then set up weekly and monthly reports that show where you rank in the search engines for your most important keywords. The reports make it easy to see how your website trends in search engines.

As long as you've built out your website correctly with the proper on-page factors (title tags, h tags, meta descriptions, etc.), if you're building quality links, developing citations, and have a proactive review acquisition system in place, you'll see your practice move up in the search results.

If you see any keywords stagnating in the report, you can go back to that keyword, figure out which website page is optimized for it, look at your links and link profile, and troubleshoot it to push that keyword to the next level.

Call Tracking

The third essential tracking mechanism that I recommend is call tracking. Having better rankings and more visits to your website is all fine and dandy, but in most businesses, nothing happens until a call is made.

Calls are crucial to your practice. You want a tracking mechanism to know how many calls are coming in monthly and what's happening within those conversations.

You want to ensure those calls are turning into booked appointments. That's what it's all about. It doesn't matter that you're in the number one position if it doesn't result in revenue for your practice. There are several call-tracking tools that you can use, such as CallRail and WhatConverts.

Most call-tracking services will let you choose a phone number based on your area code. You'll enter the area code you want the number to be, and you're given a list of available phone numbers to choose from. It's a nominal monthly fee ($1 - $5 per month), and you get a tracking number you can use on your website.

It's a forwarding number, so when someone dials it, the call will be forwarded to ring your regular office line. Some call tracking tools will also provide you with attribution information, which is detailed data that shows you where the caller found your med spa online. Knowing the number of calls your med spa was getting when you started versus the number after you incorporated your new marketing strategy is extremely powerful.

These are the essential types of tracking I recommend. You can do many different things, but analytics, keyword tracking, and call tracking give you the most critical key performance indicators to gauge your progress.

Key Performance Indicators (KPIs) for Digital Marketing

Digital marketing for med spas relies on various key performance indicators (KPIs) to measure the effectiveness and success of your marketing efforts. KPIs should be adjusted to measure the most relevant outcomes to your goals. That being said, I believe some general KPIs for digital marketing in the med spa industry are especially important. Let's briefly go over each metric.

Conversion Rate: The conversion rate measures the percentage of website visitors who take a desired action, such as booking an appointment or submitting a contact form. A high conversion rate indicates that the marketing strategies effectively drive visitors to become leads or clients.

Return on Investment (ROI): ROI measures the profitability of digital marketing campaigns by comparing the investment cost to the revenue generated. It helps assess the financial impact and effectiveness of marketing efforts and provides insights into the overall profitability of digital marketing activities.

Cost per Acquisition (CPA): CPA measures the average cost of acquiring a new client or patient. It calculates the total marketing spend divided by the number of new clients acquired within a specific period. A lower CPA indicates efficient marketing campaigns, effective allocation of resources, and likely good sales techniques that help you or your staff close more sales.

Cost per Lead (CPL): CPL measures the average cost to acquire a new lead. This valuable metric can help you calculate your marketing campaigns' cost-effectiveness. Tracking your CPL over time allows you to see how it is trending and adjust as needed.

Website Traffic: Website traffic measures the number of visitors to a med spa's website. It helps evaluate the effectiveness of various marketing channels, campaigns, and content strategies in driving user engagement and attracting potential clients.

Engagement Metrics: Engagement metrics, such as time spent on site, bounce rate, and page views per session, provide insights into how users interact with a med spa's website. Higher engagement metrics indicate that visitors find the content valuable and actively explore the website.

Social Media Engagement: Social media engagement metrics, including likes, comments, shares, and follower growth, reflect the level of audience interaction with the med spa's social media content. Strong engagement metrics demonstrate an active and interested social media following.

Email Marketing Metrics: Email marketing metrics, such as open rate, click-through rate (CTR), and conversion rate, gauge the effectiveness of email campaigns in engaging recipients and driving desired actions. High open and click-through rates indicate engaging content, while a high conversion rate suggests effective calls to action and personalized offers.

Online Reviews & Ratings: Monitoring and analyzing online reviews and ratings on platforms like Google, Yelp, and social media provide insights into client satisfaction, brand reputation, and the effectiveness of customer service efforts. Positive reviews and high ratings contribute to building trust and attracting new clients.

Search Engine Rankings: Tracking search engine rankings for targeted keywords helps assess a med spa's website's visibility and organic search performance. Higher rankings indicate improved visibility and increased chances of attracting organic traffic.

Client Lifetime Value (CLV): CLV measures the total revenue generated from a client over their lifetime as a customer of the med spa. It helps assess the long-term profitability of client relationships and highlights the importance of client retention and satisfaction.

Using analytics to gather data is just the first step. If you're not using that data to make intelligent decisions for your marketing strategy and practice, you're missing out on the true value of the data. Ensure you're gaining insights to drive action. It's what you do with the data that will result in the growth of your practice.

CHAPTER 17

STAYING COMPLIANT WITH EMAIL & SMS REGULATIONS

I felt like I needed to include a chapter on the legalities around your marketing because there is a lot of confusion around this topic. Of course, I'm not an attorney, so this isn't legal advice but an overview of some legal aspects I think you should be aware of. At the end of this chapter, I've provided links to reputable resources where you can learn more.

Protecting Patient Privacy

We can all agree that protecting patient privacy and data is paramount. When it comes to digital marketing, med spas must be incredibly diligent in complying with data protection laws, such as the Health Insurance Portability and Accountability Act (HIPAA).

To ensure compliance with HIPAA and other relevant data protection laws, you must take several critical measures if you're using digital marketing in your med spa.

First and foremost, you must obtain explicit consent from patients before using their contact information for marketing purposes. This consent should be clear, unambiguous, and opt-in-based. Ideally, you'll have a timestamp record of this consent to demonstrate compliance.

You must also implement robust security measures to safeguard patient data during email and SMS marketing campaigns. This involves using encrypted communication channels and secure servers to prevent unauthorized access to patient information. This sounds complicated, but if you're using a HIPAA-compliant email and SMS marketing platform, they've got this covered.

When sending marketing communications via email or SMS, never include any sensitive medical details in your marketing messages, even if patients have previously disclosed this information. Instead, keep marketing content focused on general promotions, offers, or educational material that doesn't reveal confidential patient health information (PHI).

By proactively complying with data protection laws and handling patient information responsibly, you're well on your way to establishing trust with your patients and demonstrating a commitment to safeguarding their privacy.

Email Marketing Legalities

I'm always surprised at how many marketers don't share details of the federal laws that pertain to email marketing. You must understand the law because you're responsible for your practice's actions, even if you're not involved with the day-to-day email marketing activities.

The Federal Trade Commission (FTC) is the US government entity that enforces the CAN-SPAM Act, a law that sets the requirements for commercial email. The penalties for non-compliance are severe. You can be penalized up to $50,120 for each separate email in violation, which was just adjusted for inflation in February 2023.

According to the FTC, the law defines commercial messages as "any electronic mail message, the primary purpose of which is the commercial advertisement or promotion of a commercial product or service."

The good news is that the law isn't complicated or hard to follow. I'm including the main requirements here; you can find more information on the FTC's website.

1. Don't use false or misleading header information.
2. Don't use deceptive subject lines.
3. Identify the message as an ad.
4. Tell recipients where you're located.
5. Tell recipients how to opt out of receiving future emails from you.
6. Honor opt-out requests promptly.
7. Monitor what others are doing on your behalf.

Many legal requirements are quickly addressed by using an email marketing service, but the need for an appropriate email marketing service is even greater for medical spas. Because medical spas may deal with PHI, your email marketing service must also be HIPAA compliant.

It may go without saying, but email blasts should never be sent directly from your regular email inbox. Besides the legal requirements not being met, there are several other reasons:

- Your Internet Service Provider (ISP) will blacklist you for sending bulk mail
- You wouldn't have any tracking metrics
- It would look unprofessional coming from your regular email

While meeting the legal requirements is important, it's also important to consider the people you're emailing. We've all dealt with annoying emails. Don't be that business. Be professional, make it easy for people to opt out, and send content that people are excited to receive.

SMS Marketing Legalities

SMS marketing, or text message marketing, is a powerful tool for businesses to engage with customers. However, there are specific legalities and regulations that marketers must be aware of to ensure compliance and avoid potential legal issues.

One of the primary legal considerations for SMS marketing is obtaining proper consent from recipients. This consent should be explicit, informed, and obtained in a manner compliant with relevant data protection laws. A few of the most popular methods are having clients opt-in by texting a keyword to a unique shortcode, filling out an online form, or signing a consent form. As mentioned earlier in this chapter, it's important to maintain records of consent as evidence of compliance in case of any future disputes.

The Telephone Consumer Protection Act (TCPA) also requires businesses to comply with other regulations. For example, companies can't send text messages before 8 am or after 9 pm unless the recipient has expressly opted in to receive messages at those times.

You also have to provide a way for consumers to opt out of receiving text messages. This can be done by including an opt-out link or keyword in every text message or allowing consumers to opt out by replying to a text message with "STOP" or "UNSUBSCRIBE."

There's recently been an upheaval in SMS marketing. In 2022, the United States began the A2P 10DLC system. "A2P" means "application to person," referring to the marketing text messages sent to consumers. This system requires businesses to register their phone numbers used for SMS marketing and get approval to send messages. The good news is that this system will improve deliverability for registered numbers and decrease deliverability for unregistered numbers. Hopefully, that means less SPAM for us all!

The bottom line is to use a reputable SMS marketing provider. A reputable SMS marketing provider will help you comply with the law and ensure your messages are delivered correctly.

Legal Policies on Your Website

In today's digital age, a website serves as the virtual storefront and primary point of interaction for businesses and organizations across the globe. While creating an engaging and user-friendly website is essential for success, many website owners overlook the significance of incorporating comprehensive legal pages.

Legal pages are crucial in establishing trust, mitigating potential risks, and ensuring legal compliance. Legal pages are so important we won't work with any medical spas that refuse to add legal pages to their website. If the law isn't enough reason, it's rumored that Google prefers websites with privacy policies, which should weigh heavily on your decision to have legal pages.

Various laws and regulations govern online activities, including data protection, consumer rights, and intellectual property. Having legal pages tailored to the specific nature of your website ensures compliance with these laws and reduces the risk of legal disputes and penalties.

For instance, if your website collects any form of user data, and a website visitor's name and email address are both considered user data, your website needs a privacy policy on your website. If your website uses tracking software, as I outlined in Chapter 16, your website needs a privacy policy. A well-crafted privacy policy outlining data collection practices and user rights is essential to meet the requirements of data protection laws. The challenge is that every state is different, and the playing field is constantly in flux as new privacy laws are voted in.

Legal pages are a clear and concise communication channel for managing user expectations. The Terms of Service outline the rules and guidelines for using the website, setting boundaries for user behavior and interactions. Similarly, a Disclaimer clarifies the scope and limitations of the website's content, products, or services, protecting the website owner from potential liabilities arising from reliance on the provided information. No matter how well-intentioned a website owner may be, legal disputes can still arise. Legal pages can protect the owner's interests and provide a strong defense in these situations. Don't worry, I have a resource for you at the end of this chapter.

Having legal pages on your website is not just a matter of legal compliance; it is a fundamental aspect of building trust, managing user expectations, and protecting your business interests. Legal pages instill confidence in visitors that their data is safe and the website operates transparently and ethically. They also serve as a vital defense in legal challenges and disputes. So, whether you are a small business owner or a large corporation, investing time and effort in creating comprehensive legal pages for your website is a prudent decision that yields significant benefits in the long run.

By playing by the rules, you not only stay out of trouble but also show you care about your client's privacy, promoting good, honest marketing in the fast-paced digital world. So, staying compliant is a win-win—keeping your med spa on the right side of the law and fostering positive relationships with your valued clients.

Resources to Learn More

The websites listed here are valuable resources to learn more about the legal aspects of med spa marketing.

US Department of Health and Human Services

https://www.hhs.gov/

Compliancy Group

https://compliancy-group.com/

Federal Trade Commission CAN-SPAM Act

https://www.ftc.gov/business-guidance/resources/can-spam-act-compliance-guide-business

Cellular Telecommunications Industry Association (CTIA)

https://www.ctia.org/

Termageddon
https://termageddon.com/

CHAPTER 18

NEXT STEPS TO FAST-TRACK YOUR MEDSPA'S MARKETING RESULTS

Throughout this book, I have shared abundant information, and I hope you've implemented it along the way.

You've mapped out your digital marketing plan and claimed and optimized your Google Maps listing. You learned how to optimize your website for the most commonly searched keywords in your area and how to leverage paid ads to get in front of potential clients who are searching for the very treatments your practice offers. We then dove into leveraging email and SMS marketing for more repeat and referral business.

If you have taken action, you're probably well on your way to seeing marketing results for your practice.

Need More Help?

If you've gotten to this point and need extra help to implement these ideas for your med spa, we're here to support you. As experts in helping medical spas nationwide, we've had tremendous success implementing these strategies.

You can contact us directly to schedule a conversation about your medspa's digital marketing. Just text "marketing" to (360) 504-4640 or visit https://gomargott.com/get-started/ to complete a brief online form.

We'll get a little information from you about your practice. Then we'll review your online presence—your website, search engine placement, social media, ad campaigns, and even your competitors. We complete an assessment that includes opportunities for improvement and let you know what you can do to take your online marketing efforts to the next level.

If you're serious about growing your med spa practice, you owe it to yourself to take me up on this offer. We'd love to work with you, but the Marketing Assessment is yours to keep either way.

To Your Success!